Courtship and Love among
the Enslaved in North Carolina

D1713215

COURTSHIP AND LOVE AMONG THE ENSLAVED IN NORTH CAROLINA

Rebecca J. Fraser

University Press of Mississippi

Jackson

Margaret Walker Alexander Series
in African American Studies

www.upress.state.ms.us

The University Press of Mississippi is a member of the
Association of American University Presses.

First printing 2007
∞

Library of Congress Cataloging-in-Publication Data

Fraser, Rebecca J., 1978–
Courtship and love among the enslaved in North Carolina /
Rebecca J. Fraser.
p.   cm. — (Margaret Walker Alexander series in
African American studies)
Includes bibliographical references and index.
ISBN-13: 978-1-934110-07-2 (cloth : alk. paper)
ISBN-10: 1-934110-07-8 (cloth : alk. paper) 1. Slaves—North
Carolina—Social life and customs—19th century. 2. Love—
North Carolina—History—19th century. 3. Courtship—North
Carolina—History—19th century. 4. Slaves—North Carolina—
Biography. 5. Couples—North Carolina—Biography. 6. African
Americans—North Carolina—Social life and customs—19th
century. 7. African Americans—North Carolina—Biography.
8. Plantation life—North Carolina—History—19th century.
9. North Carolina—Social life and customs—19th century.
10. North Carolina—Biography. I. Title.
E445.N8F73 2007
306.73′4086250975609034—dc22
2007014886

British Library Cataloging-in-Publication Data available

For Derek

Contents

Acknowledgments

THIS BOOK WOULD probably never have begun, and definitely would never have been finished, if it were not for the persistence and motivation of Rebecca Earle and Cecily Jones. They have both cast critical eyes over every aspect of this research when it was in its embryonic form, and I am forever thankful that they forced me to constantly question, reconsider, and revise my thoughts—I have come to realize that this is a necessary and valuable, although extremely painful, aspect of any research project. For your intellectual stimulation and for encouraging my insights I offer you my thanks.

This research has been enriched by valuable conversations and seminar discussions with numerous members of staff and students located at the University of East Anglia, Warwick, and York. Special thanks are given to Emily West, Tim Lockley, and Henrice Altink, who have provided thoughtful and reflective encouragement throughout the writing of this book. I also want to thank John David Smith and Charles Joyner for forcing me to reflect more critically on my analysis and to develop a deeper empathy with those I was researching.

So many people have left their mark on me throughout my life and none more than individuals who through their love of teaching are able to change the way people think about themselves and the world they live in. Carol Miles was one such woman. It is a bitter irony that those such as Carol, who have so many important and valuable things to say, are taken away from us far too soon. Her ability to face everything that life threw at her was an inspiration to all who had the privilege of meeting her. I know that Carol would have thought that this reference to her was "bloody soft," but she'd be secretly chuffed that one of her students had made it this far. This book is my proof that I listened to what she said and have never rested on my laurels.

I seemed to have spent most of my time during my research visits to North Carolina bothering archivists for some reason or another. The staff and graduate students at Duke's Rare Book, Manuscript and Special Collections Library and the Southern Historical Collection at the University of North Carolina were a crucial and invaluable aid for a young and inexperienced researcher such as myself. This research would also not have been possible without a generous scholarship from the Arts and Humanities Research Council.

I want to express my thanks to Craig Gill, editor-in-chief at the University Press of Mississippi, for his faith in my work and to managing editor Anne Stascavage and editorial assistant Valerie Jones. Special thanks are also extended to copyeditor Angelique Cain whose care and attention to detail guided this book through to the finish line.

Andrew and Carol Griffin, my mother and father, have provided unstinting emotional support and encouragement throughout. Martyn Griffin, thank you for the additional copyediting and for managing to read the majority of the manuscript. Despite our disciplines being distinctly different you had the fortitude and intellectual capability to encourage me to expand my thoughts and think harder about my analysis.

To my husband, Derek Fraser, to whom I dedicate this book, thank you for putting up with the tears and the tantrums and the desperate tapping of the keyboard during the early hours of the morning. Perhaps your sleep pattern (and mine) will return to some normalcy now. Through the highs and the lows you have always sustained your faith in me and my ability to get the job done. You have also always managed to put a smile on my face and have made sure that I don't lose touch with what's truly important (namely soccer and beer!).

Some of the arguments used in this book have already appeared in article form elsewhere. I am extremely grateful to *Slavery and Abolition* and the *Journal of Southern History* for allowing me to republish them here. For further information see, "Goin' Back Over There to See That Girl: Competing Spaces in the Social World of the Enslaved In Antebellum North Carolina," *Slavery and Abolition*, 25 (April 2004), pp. 94–113, available at http://www.tandf.co.uk/journals; and "Courtship Contests and the Meaning of Conflict in the Folklore of Slaves," *Journal of Southern History*, LXXI, (Nov 2005), pp. 769–802.

Courtship and Love among the Enslaved in North Carolina

Introduction

"I'VE HEARD SOME of the young people laugh about slave love, but they should envy the love which kept mother and father so close together in life and even held them in death."[1] Alonzo Haywood's comment reflected on the relationship between his father, Willis Haywood, and his mother, Mirana Denson, who were both enslaved in antebellum North Carolina.[2] He explained that while his father was enslaved at Falls of Neuse, he fell in love with Mirana Denson, who lived in Raleigh, "He come to see her ever' chance he got and then they were married." Reflecting on the strength and sincerity of his parent's feelings for one another he commented, "Mother died near twenty years ago and father died four years later. He had not cared to live since mother left him."[3]

Alonzo Haywood was interviewed during the 1930s in the former slaveholding state of North Carolina for the Works Progress Administration (WPA) project. The prevailing view among historians and white North American society in general at this time was that sexual relationships between slaves had been promiscuous, casual, and invested with little real emotional meaning. Such was the portrayal of slave life and the characterization of slave men and women in the American South that they were deemed to have been incapable of falling in love or establishing relationships that were predicated around feelings of affection, intimacy, or tenderness.

Yet, as illustrated in the words of Alonzo Haywood and countless others evidenced within the pages of this book, enslaved love was not to be ridiculed or laughed about. The enslaved were able to create and maintain relationships that were grounded in particular ideals that resisted slaveholders' definitions of these relationships. They worked strenuously within and around the power structures shaping their lives to maintain their courtships and romantic affairs.[4] These relationships were formed in various places and spaces, sometimes under the direct observance of the slaveholder in the context of the working day of the enslaved. At other times they were created in social spaces which the enslaved defined as their own. These particular spaces could have included those of an illicit nature, such as secret frolics staged away from the defined boundaries of the plantation. It would have also included the quarters of the enslaved, their own domestic spaces, where couples would have shared laughter and tears, joy and anger, sorrow and joy, with another who was best placed to understand. These were the private and intimate spaces shared between enslaved couples, within which they were able to recognize their own and each other's personhood, their values and qualities as men and women.

By engaging in these relationships enslaved men and women ran deep risks as they confronted and challenged the slave system in significant ways. The forms that these challenges took would be understood in contemporary scholarship as *passive* or *everyday forms* of resistance as opposed to outright rebellion or insurrection.[5] Although the enslaved would not have differentiated between the two as they struggled against the inhumanities of the slave system on a daily basis, these definitions have proved invaluable to current scholarship focusing upon enslaved life in the slaveholding South. They have allowed historians to broaden the margins of what can be usefully considered as resistance. Through their courting relationships then, the enslaved demonstrated their resistance to a system that served to deny them their very personhood and in the process gave shape to their emotional worlds.

Courtship has had a somewhat "strange career and a dubious standing in the study of family history." Among scholarly discussions concerning the enslaved, it has usually been somewhat submerged in a broader study of marriage, family, and the household. Although more recently academics have contributed significant discussions of enslaved courtship to the historiography, there still remains the need for a more in-depth and sustained consideration of this aspect of enslaved life,[6] one within which courtship is understood as more than a "mere passage instead of its own social event."[7]

By the antebellum period slavery had become institutionalized across the American South. The enslaved were subject to increasing restrictions that regulated their mobility and behavior. Furthermore, the slaveholder was concerned in controlling all aspects of enslaved life, especially that of sexual unions, which were central to the overall organization of the plantation and reproduction of their labor force.[8] Nevertheless, the enslaved themselves sought to define the nature and shape of their own courtship experiences. These relationships provided an opportunity for enslaved men and women to occupy identities that were distinct from that of "slave," embodying roles such as companion, confidante, helpmate, and soulmate. However, they also posed problems and the very real potential of conflict within enslaved communities as men and women vied for each other's affections; hearts were broken, jealousies were voiced, and objections were raised.

In fundamental ways then, courtship represented an arena of contestation between the enslaved themselves as much as between the enslaved and the slaveholder. Apparently, however, the active pursuit of such relationships on the part of enslaved men and women highlights their fundamental importance. Their courtships should be understood as landscapes upon which they fought for degrees of emotional autonomy both within the institution of slavery and within their own communities.

Although love and emotions have been absent from much of the historical analysis concerning the enslaved in the South, the enslaved have also been neglected in the historiography of love and emotions. This neglect is especially evident when one considers the wealth of material relating to the development of romantic love on the North American mainland and the historical attention that has been given to the courtship practices of the white elite.[9]

Nevertheless, what love and courtship meant for the enslaved, both in memory and in practice, was a common theme in their recollections. In her autobiography, the formerly enslaved Harriet Jacobs posed the question, "Why does the slave ever love? Why allow the tendrils of the heart to twine around objects which may at any moment be wrenched away by the hand of violence?" Indeed, falling in love for the enslaved was fraught with immense emotional and physical difficulties, as Jacobs was well aware. Having fallen in love with a local free black man, whom she describes as having loved with "all the ardor of a young girl's first love," he proposed to buy her freedom and then marry her. Jacobs knew that her master, Dr. Flint, however, would never agree. He was "too wilful and arbitrary a man to consent to that arrangement." Subject to Dr. Flint's sexual advances toward her, she resolved that the situation was hopeless and she convinced her lover that "[f]or *his* sake . . . I ought not to link his own fate with my unhappy destiny. . . . The dream of my girlhood was over. I felt lonely and desolate."[10]

Nevertheless, the majority of the enslaved did love. They allowed their hearts to become entwined with another, no matter the actual realities that threatened their relationships. Indeed, it was perhaps the enslaved who were best placed to understand this need for love and affection. The formerly enslaved Thomas H. Jones made this acute observation when he wrote:

> It seems to me that no one can have such fondness of love, and such intensity of desire for home and home affections, as the poor slave. Despised and trampled upon by a cruel race of unfeeling men, the bondman must die in the prime of his wretched life, if he finds no refuge in a dear home, where love and sympathy shall meet him from hearts made sacred to him by his own irrepressible affection and tenderness for them.[11]

The enslaved attempted to negotiate a path to their lover's door, both metaphorically and literally. As they did so they came up against numerous obstacles that they were forced to overcome. The slaveholder and the mechanics of power built into the slave system were instrumental in this process.

After 1808 and the outlawing of the transatlantic slave trade to Africa, the sexual unions that the enslaved created became of extreme significance in the management of the plantation. Enslaved men and women's ability to reproduce "good stock" was paramount to the slaveholders' continuing success and profitable returns. Katie Darling, who was born a slave in Texas in 1849, argued that "Niggers don't court then like they do now. Massa pick out a portly man and a portly gal and just put 'em together. What he want am the stock."[12] Clara Jones remembered that when she got married in 1860 her master, Felton McGee of Wake County, North Carolina, reminded her "dat dere duty wus ter have a houseful of chilluns fer him."[13]

The complex dynamics of power and control, central to mastery in the Old South, thus posed particular problems for enslaved men and women who were involved in a courting relationship and who would have seen their first "duty" as being to one another. Similarly, Willie McCullough, who was born just after emancipation in 1869 in Darlington County, South Carolina, recalled the story that his mother, Rilla, had told him about her master's policies regarding the selection of slave coupling. "Mother told me that when she became a woman at the age of 16 years her master went to a slave owner near by and got a six-foot nigger man, almost an entire stranger to her, and told her she must marry him. . . . The slave owners treated them as if they had been common animals in this respect."[14]

Indeed, because of the systems of regulation and control manifest in the southern slave system by the antebellum period, some among the enslaved refused to get involved in a romantic relationship. As the formerly enslaved Julie Woodberry commented, "I ain't never married cause you had to court on de sly in dat day en time."[15] Thomas Hall declared that "Gettin' married and havin' a family was a joke in the days of slavery."[16] These systems of control were not consistent throughout the southern states, however, or even in one particular state, differing, for example, between slaveholders themselves; urban and rural environments; or the police measures in the county. However, the various measures employed across the slaveholding states could leave the enslaved having to risk life and limb to see their loved ones.

Mary A. Bell recalled how very difficult it was just for her mother and father, who were enslaved in Missouri, to see each other, as they lived on different plantations. "My father was not allowed to come to see my mother but two nights a week. Dat was Wednesday and Saturday. So often he came home all bloody from beatings his old nigger overseer would give him." In a scenario that was undoubtedly familiar to enslaved children across the South, Mary remembered how her mother "would take these bloody clothes off of him, bathe the sore places and grease them good and wash and iron his clothes so he could go back clean."[17]

Sometimes, the pain, loneliness, and horror were too much to take. Annie Tate's grandmother, who was enslaved to the Jones family of Wake County, North Carolina, killed herself after her slaveholder sold her husband to a trader from Mississippi. This was following a fight between the overseer and Annie's grandpa that resulted in the death of the former. Annie recounted the story handed down to her by her mother of how the master made several of the other slaves hold her grandpa while he whipped him. She explained how "[h]e cuts his back all ter pieces an' den he throws him in de barn, chained down ter de flo'." Annie's grandmother stole out to see her husband, chained to the floor of a barn, whispering through the cracks in the wall to offer solace and comfort. After he was sold, Annie recollected, "Pore gran'maw am nigh bout crazy so she walks off'en de plantation. Down on de aidge of de plantation runs de Neuse so gran'maw gits dar, an' jumps in."[18]

The weeping wounds of slavery were left to the patient care and unrelenting love of a tender devotion and heartfelt understanding. This must have been coupled with a shared sense of horror at the inhumanities of the system that they had been forced to live in. Sometimes the anguish of witnessing a loved one being mercilessly subjected to horrific pain and severe abuse, feeling every stroke of the whip and every shriek of agony, feeling helpless, hopeless, and lifeless coupled with the utter devastation of sale and subsequent separation could be too much for one heart to take.

Of course, the enslaved were not just subject to the regulatory measures of the slaveholder or the system of slavery where their courtships were concerned. This was a relationship which took place primarily in the thick realities of enslaved community life, within and around enslaved households.[19] Thus, their relationships were also subject to factors such as control, competition, and conflict originating from within the enslaved community. Jealousy, competition, and contests over courtships among enslaved men and women themselves would have been keenly felt in a community of individuals who were already experiencing the threat of violence and conflict on a daily basis at the hands of their enslavers. Such manifestations *within* the quarters of the enslaved therefore could pose serious ramifications for the concept of a "community." Dylan C. Penningroth has recently called attention to the dynamics of community among the enslaved, arguing that scholars need to think much more seriously about how they "interpret evidence of neglect and loneliness in the 'negro quarters.'" The emphasis in past scholarship on conflict between whites and blacks has "tend[ed] to obscure the experience of black people, whose understanding of economic and social life involved far more than their relations with white people."[20]

According to the narratives of the formerly enslaved, jealousy was particularly apparent when a man had a wife or lover who lived on another plantation. Caleb Craig, who was enslaved in South Carolina, stated that if a man had a wife who resided elsewhere that he would "see little peace or happiness. He could see de wife once a week, in a pass, and jealousy kep' him 'stracted de balance of de week, if he love her very much."[21] The possible advantages and disadvantages posed by a crossplantation relationship for the enslaved have been the subject of academic debate in previous years. Some argue that, although "jealousies and suspicions were hard to deal with at a distance," at least they were shielded from "the misery of witnessing each other's abuse."[22] This particular argument has some validity if we recall such examples as Mary Bell's mother and father or Annie Tate's grandparents. However, as another scholar of slavery points out, "If slave husbands were on the home place, masters may have had less compulsion to whip married slave women who would have felt much safer having their husbands on the place."[23]

Living under the regime of southern slavery meant that the enslaved had little, if any, choice about where they actually physically lived. They had to just make the best out of an impossible situation where their courtships and romances were concerned. The trick may well have been "to be selective and then fall in love," but affairs of the heart are never that simple for any of us, throughout different cultures, time periods, and geographical locations.[24] We can rarely choose who we fall in love with, and consequently we must face the complexities of the situation as it presents itself to us in all its glorious, heart-wrenching, joyful, and painful forms.

Some among the formerly enslaved recalled love as something which was not for them. "Colored people don't pay no 'tention to what white folks call love," Jane Johnson argued. She did, however, relate to her interviewer for the WPA project that she had "married dat man of mine, Tillghman Thompson, and us got 'long right smart, 'till he died. I got another one, Anderson Johnson, and he die too, so here I is, left here yit."[25] Despite her protestations to the contrary, Jane Johnson had evidently found something of worth in her first relationship to have wanted to marry again. It would seem that, much as in any community of individuals, there were competing definitions of what love was or what courtship entailed. Nevertheless, the desire to love and be loved in return is an inherent feeling common to all across countless different places for time immemorial. The ways in which we choose to express that need, in words and actions, differ with each individual and are determined by factors as wide-ranging as cultural imperatives, individual personalities, and legislative measures, for example. But it is to a certain extent the questions of who we love and why we love them that give shape to what we do in our lives and make us the people that we are.

The choice of North Carolina as the slaveholding state which this research chooses to focus upon might, at first glance, appear illogical. The state held few slaves in comparison to its neighbors, South Carolina and Virginia, and some commentators have even suggested that slavery was somewhat milder in form here then elsewhere in the antebellum South and consequently "los[t] much of its inhumanity."[26] However, it occupies a distinct location in the history of slaveholding states in the American South, and some interesting questions can be posed relating to the ways in which the enslaved in this particular state participated in practices of courtship and expressed their love for another. Although

American slavery across the South was, "above all, a system of economic exploitation, racial formation, and racial domination," the ways in which this system of slavery operated were influenced by numerous factors to do with *where* it operated.[27] From long established states on the eastern seaboard to frontier societies in the West to the deep South, from state to state and even within states, from urban dwellings and so-called domestic slavery to rural plantations and farms and field work, they all produced their own distinct versions of slavery that may have shared certain characteristics across space but were distinct precisely because of the place that they operated. Considering the ways in which different work practices shaped enslaved courting relationships is key to this discussion. Cultivating sugar cane in Louisiana, for example, would have necessitated different courting practices than if the enslaved worked on a turpentine plantation in eastern North Carolina.

Slavery in North Carolina was distinct as a system, varying across the region because of the crops cultivated. In terms of the cultural lives of the enslaved, the crop they cultivated could have direct influence upon the amount of time they could steal back for themselves in which to pursue a courtship. Characterized by regional diversity across the state, the enslaved experience must have been particularly varied. They were heavily concentrated in those areas that were dependent on labor intensive crops and produce. For example, Halifax County, located in the northern tobacco belt of the state, had a slave population that was nearly double that of its white population by the antebellum period. In 1830, its white population numbered 5,870, and its slave population was counted as 9,790. In comparison, during the same year Buncombe County, which lay in the far western region of the state and whose economy was based around subsistence farming, had a white population of 14,494 and a slave population of only 1,572.[28]

The number of slaveholders concentrated in particular areas gradually increased as cotton began to emerge as the leading staple crop in many North Carolinian counties, especially in those areas south of the tobacco belt in the Piedmont and along the Coastal plain. The growth of cotton production on an extensive scale in the state combined with the increased number of settlements in the uplands and the growth of coastal plantations created strong slaveholding areas in numerous regions.[29] The enslaved populations in these areas began to rapidly increase as local white farmers became increasingly dependent on the labor intensive crop of cotton and consequently required the type of labor force that the system of slavery could offer. By the 1830s cotton was a prosperous crop grown in many sections of North Carolina, and it emerged as a staple crop in the eastern counties of Edgecombe, Bertie, Pitt, Martin, and Lenoir and the southwestern counties of Mecklenburg, Iredell, Anson, and Richmond. Tobacco cultivation was confined to the northern Piedmont counties along the Virginian border, and eastern North Carolina retained its image as the turpentine belt. In the northeast large plantations flourished producing wheat and corn for export. The coastal regions of New Hanover and Brunswick continued to cultivate rice as their staple crop.[30]

Slaveholders in areas such as the Cape Fear region to the south, the Piedmont in central North Carolina, and the Albemarle Sound along the northern coastal plain, cultivated labor intensive crops and thus demanded large slave workforces. In these places developed a white slaveholding elite whose wealth was derived from their sizeable slave labor force and the profitable returns made on the export of specific crops. This elite group of slaveholders typically held more than fifty slaves and included men such as Charles Pettigrew of Washington County, who owned 157 slaves in 1850.[31] However, there existed in North Carolina few of the huge columned mansions that dotted the landscape of South Carolina during this period. In fact, in comparison to the neighboring states of South Carolina and Virginia, the majority of plantations and slaveholdings in North Carolina were considered small, and the state was popularly characterized as Rip Van Winkle during the antebellum era. "During her heavy slumber she has, like Rip Van Winkle, grown poor and ragged."[32] Upon visiting, members of the white elite from other states generally agreed with this characterization. In 1853, Sarah F. Hicks moved to North Carolina from New York following her marriage to Dr. Benjamin Williams. In a letter to her parents, she wrote that "I find my wardrobe quite too extravagant. . . . You have no idea how entirely different everything here is. If you call Long Island behind the time, I don't know what you would call North Carolina. It has been rightly termed Rip Van Winkle."[33]

Because of the relative smallness of plantations in North Carolina many of the enslaved lived and worked together in restricted communities, severely limiting their options when it came to the question of courtship. For example, in 1850, only 91 slaveholders in the state owned more than 100 slaves. By 1860 331,059 slaves were held in the entire state. This figure was comparatively low compared to Virginia and South Carolina in the same year, where slaves numbered 490,865 and 402,406 respectively.[34] To meet, socialize, and court other members of the enslaved community the enslaved were often forced to look beyond their immediate surroundings and the confines of the plantation. Their social worlds often moved between and across plantations, and recollections from the formerly enslaved in this state suggest that this was how enslaved men and women typically managed their courtships.[35] Enslaved men and women were obliged to engage in crossplantation unions because of the relatively small size of the plantations. Unequal sex ratios between them further compounded such problems. Men initially dominated among the enslaved in the early colonial history of the state, but the sex ratio significantly decreased as the period progressed. From 1751 to 1755 the sex ratio was about 153 enslaved men for every 100 enslaved women. From 1761 to 1775 this number decreased to around 125 men for every 100 women.[36] This imbalance in the sex ratio was subject to regional variation, and the more densely settled areas of North Carolina experienced much more favorable sex ratios. Thus, for the enslaved who inhabited areas in North Carolina where there were large plantations, the opportunities to meet and establish relationships with members of the opposite sex were greatly increased. However, for those who did not the opportunities for courtship were somewhat more complex.

At this point it is probably pertinent to comment on the methodological questions framing this research. Exploring the intimate lives of those who inhabited the past is difficult. Personal texts, such as letters and diaries, reveal much to the historian concerned with exploring the private worlds of particular individuals, but they are also beset by methodological problems relating to subjectivity and interpretation. As Peter Stearns and Jan Lewis underline, "[w]hat makes the study of emotions so stimulating and yet so maddening is the elusiveness of its subject; the knowledge that we can, in fact, never be entirely confident that our interpretations are correct. The shifting sands of human emotion and experience both bedevil and beguile us."[37]

In contrast to historical analysis that focuses on observable events, the history of emotions is much more difficult to understand and interpret because of their nonphysical nature. "We have a few old mouth-to-mouth tales; we exhume from old trunks and boxes and drawers letters without salutation or signature, in which men and women who once breathed are now merely initials or nicknames out of some now incomprehensible affection which sound to us like Sanskrit or Chocktaw."[38] Faulkner also considers the thought processes that attend the historical examination of such sources, "carefully, the paper old and faded and falling to pieces, the writing faded, almost indecipherable, yet meaningful, familiar in shape and sense, the name and presence of volatile and sentient forces; you bring them together in the proportions called for, but nothing happens; you re-read, tedious and intent, poring, making sure that you have forgotten nothing, made no miscalculation; you bring them together again and again nothing happens: just the words, the symbols, the shapes themselves, shadowy inscrutable and serene."[39] To a certain extent this is true of all sources employed by the historian, which are selected and shaped by a particular social context and a governing consensus. However, it is particularly apparent when researching the emotional dimensions of the past that historians are required to ask different sorts of questions of the source material available.

For those interested in the emotional lives of the enslaved the task becomes even more problematic. Few personal texts are available that truly reveal the intimate lives of the enslaved. Legally forbidden to learn to read and write, only a minority of enslaved men and women were able to master the written word and thus give expression to their emotions through this particular form. As Larry Hudson points out, researching the nature of love, courtship, and familial bonds among the enslaved is particularly difficult because there are few sources available in which the formerly enslaved really get to the heart of the matter, "the

scarcity of accounts that directly attest to the affection between slave couples . . .
should be viewed more as a reflection of the slaves' reluctance to behave openly
in the public world than as an indication of an absence of such affection."[40]
Their voices are somewhat muted or silenced in the sources, making the task
of reconstructing that experience problematic. Because the enslaved largely inhabited a nonliterate community, the historian must turn to the verbal aspect of
enslaved culture, the "collective created vernacular history of enslavement," to
unearth any sense of the emotional structures of enslaved life.[41] The most important sources providing historians of slavery within the United States with the
most detailed evidence regarding enslaved life are the Works Progress Administration (WPA) narratives. They have, however, been subject to some of the most
severe criticism concerning their validity as historical sources.

More than two thousand interviews compiled in seventeen states, the WPA
narratives should be considered "a unique and illuminating source of information not only about the institution of slavery but about the psychology of the
enslaved as well."[42] B. A. Botkin, folklore editor of the Federal Writers' project, argues that the collective memories contained in the WPA narratives did not
have to be understood as *true life histories*. He suggests that they should instead
be seen as a "kind of legendary history of one's life and times, which furnishes
unconscious evidence for the historian."[43] Historians have, however, approached
the WPA narratives with much more caution than Botkin had envisaged. Some
have questioned the validity of the narratives and their reliability as a source representative of the life of the enslaved in the slaveholding South. Many historians have asked whether the age of the respondents affected their memories of
slavery and point to the length of time that had elapsed since most of those interviewed had been emancipated (at least seventy years) as another factor that
may have influenced their memories of enslavement. Others have criticized the
WPA narratives on the basis of the artificial nature of the interviewing situation in which they took place and point in particular to the prevalence of white
male interviewers on the project, which might have shaped and distorted the response of black interviewees.

For many, the main difficulty in using the WPA narratives with any confi-
dence is the issue of memory. Donna Spindel argues that the interviews raise a
number of evidentiary concerns and that the most troublesome "hinge on the
reliability of long term memory."[44] She points out that at the time of the interviews, these men and women ranged in age from 72 years to 108 years old and
that at least two thirds of the respondents were more than 80 years old. She also
suggests that the majority of those interviewed had limited access to education
and literacy, which could have had detrimental effects on their capacity to recall remote events, especially as they were being asked to recollect memories of
events that had taken place over seventy years previously. Thus, Spindel con-

cludes that the narratives were highly unreliable as a true testimony of the life of the enslaved.

Paul Escott claims, however, that there is no necessary connection between an individual's age and their memory. He wrote that "memories are fallible, and in the 1930s the former slaves were recalling events of seventy or eighty years before. . . . [I]t is also true that the brain records and preserves the events of an individual's life and that older people often dwell more in memory than the young."[45] Escott also points to the fact that many of the events that the interviewees were asked to recall were pivotal moments in their lives—marriage, sale and separation, freedom—thus it was more likely that people would remember clearly events that were significant in their lives and that held meaning for them.

To counter Spindel's argument concerning the consequences of the lack of formal education in the lives of the enslaved, we might employ B. A. Botkin's contention that "[i]n the bookless world, memory takes the place of history and biography."[46] Literacy did become increasingly significant among the enslaved over the course of the early nineteenth century, but the culture of the enslaved was largely one in which the vernacular took precedence over the written word. The enslaved constructed a vernacular history of enslavement, "a narrative about the past constructed by laypeople in their everyday tongue"[47] and as such recalled events that were distant or remote by interpreting oral lore rather than by revising the written word.

Escott, however, argues that, rather than the issue of memory, "the most formidable problem encountered in using the narratives is the problem of candour."[48] Racial etiquette in the post-emancipation south demanded that the black men and women remain subservient to the white population, and this was observed in the interviewing processes employed for the WPA project. As the majority of interviewers were local white men, often from former slaveholding families, the response of the formerly enslaved interviewees was no doubt shaped by former power relations embedded in the southern slave system.

John Blassingame was particularly critical of this element of the narratives and it was perhaps central to his decision not to include them within his influential text, *The Slave Community*.[49] Blassingame argues that the interview situation was not conducive to accurate communication and recording between white interviewers and black respondents. He claims that only in the specific states where black interviewers were used, such as Florida, could the historian gain anything reliable from the collection. The conditions in 1930s America—the Great Depression, poverty, and high unemployment, especially among the African American community—meant that the interviews took place within a situation of dependency and racism. Blassingame thus asserts that "the answers to many of the questions on the WPA interview schedule could neither be divorced from the dependent position of the aged blacks nor the contemporary state of race relations in the South."[50]

White interviewers lacked empathy with their formerly enslaved respondents. Their view of the slave system was usually from the standpoint of the slaveholder, especially as many of the local whites who conducted the interviews were related to former slaveholders in the county. In some states, the most renowned being Mississippi, editors would revise certain interviews before sending them off to the national office in Washington, D.C. According to Sharon Ann Musher, however, this revision was atypical of the state editors in most areas, and only in six states did they revise interviews before sending them on. The interviews that were conducted in North Carolina were not revised before being sent to Washington.[51]

Black respondents in turn were therefore naturally cautious and guarded in their answers. Yet as Edward E. Baptist points out, many of those being interviewed for this project related stories which could not have sounded complimentary to white ears, and sometimes especially not to those whites conducting the interviews. In fact, as Baptist points out, "some ex-slaves were directly confrontational. And while these interviewees were near the end of their days, for some human beings those years became the peak of moral courage. Time grew short, there is little left to lose, and the cost of being silent became clearer."[52]

Blassingame argues that by employing white women, as opposed to white men, and black instead of white interviewers, the project attempted to overcome this problem.[53] White women had less access to formal methods of power and control than their male counterparts possessed and as such may not have posed the same threat to southern black men and women. The black community was perhaps more willing to provide honest answers without fear of reprisals. Several scholars have also argued that statistical surveys reveal that the formerly enslaved who talked to black interviewers were far more willing to reveal the internal dynamics of enslaved life than those who were interviewed by white project workers.[54]

In the North Carolina narratives, 60 percent of respondents were interviewed by women,[55] yet none of the seven interviewers were black.[56] The dynamics of power inherent within any interview situation leave us in a quandary. Should the North Carolina narratives be understood as more representative or reliable because of the presence of white women on the interviewing staff? Even though white southern women were excluded from more formal routes of power, they were nevertheless part of the southern power nexus, and many were probably the descendants of slaveholders in the local area. Thus, their presence on the interviewing staff in North Carolina may have done little to remedy the problems outlined above.

We might also question whether the possible advantage of white southern women on the interviewing staff in North Carolina was outweighed or negated by the absence of black interviewers listed as WPA project workers? Even if black interviewers had been involved in the collection of the North Carolina narratives it is naïve to assume that this would have eradicated all of the power dynamics that structured the context of an interview situation. We can only assume that black interviewers did not represent a threat to their elderly, rural, and formerly enslaved respondents. Although college-educated southern blacks may have represented a positive symbol of progress to the formerly enslaved, it is also a feasible argument that many among the elderly black community may have viewed these men and women with a degree of caution. Some may, for example, have resented the younger generation for adopting mainstream, white values and making use of white institutions to escape their black roots.

In addition, the formerly enslaved may have felt ashamed to reveal parts of their past to this younger generation of African Americans. After all, during slavery many would have been forced to stand and watch, able to do very little, while a loved one was mercilessly beaten, tortured, and on occasion sexually exploited. There surely would have been a certain level of resistance on the part of the formerly enslaved to reveal to younger members of their own race that they had been powerless in these traumatic circumstances. Unable to stand up for their loved ones, would they have chosen not to tell these stories in their full details to African American interviewers, chosen not to reveal these incidents in their truly horrific and complex forms for fear of being judged? In comparison, the formerly enslaved may not have been so reluctant to express their anger, grief, and heartache to the children of those who had inflicted such pain. There are complex and contradictory power dynamics to consider when dealing with the WPA narratives, and therefore it is debatable whether the college-educated black man and woman may have been any more knowable than the local white southerner.

Many of the critiques of the WPA collection focus upon the question of whether the narratives accurately reflect the more brutal aspects of slavery, such as whippings and punishments. David Bailey claims that the WPA narratives are unreliable because they can only reflect on the life of an enslaved child rather than on the conditions and experiences of the adult enslaved in the American South. He argues that the WPA narratives can not be trusted as historical sources because the view of slavery that they illustrate is through the eyes of children who had not suffered the indignities and brutalities of the slave system to the same degree as the adult men and women enslaved in the American South.[57] C. Vann Woodward concurs with this argument and writes, "The slave experience of the majority was, in fact, mainly that of childhood, a period before the full rigors and worst aspects of the slave discipline were typically felt and a period more likely than others to be favorably colored in the memory of the aged."[58]

It is important to recall that the narratives were compiled as part of a project concerning American folklore as a whole rather than slavery per se. Bailey argues

that the recollections contained in the narratives are mainly childhood memories
of enslavement, but this interpretation ignores the strong oral traditions and the
crafting of a vernacular history that persisted among African American communities following emancipation. Many of the tales told in the collection do not
concern the storyteller directly but are stories that have been told and retold to
them concerning their parents, grandparents, close friends, or relatives. Within
communities that were forbidden to learn to read or write, the spoken word was
given much more significance, as was the ability to remember a story and recount
it with meaning and depth.

Primarily in response to certain scholars' refusal to use the WPA narratives
as valid source material, George Rawick, who edited the published version of the
collection, questions why one source has to be rated superior or inferior to another. There is, he argues, "a serious departure from logic, fairness and coherence
in the views of leading scholars of American slavery who have reservations about
the slave narrative as sources and who prefer the diaries of planters, fugitive slave
advertisements, and essays on the management of slaves published in southern
agricultural periodicals."[59] The tendency in past scholarship had been to make
use of sources originating from the elite white southern community to explain
the dynamics of the slave system. Rawick argued that while the WPA narratives
did have their own distortions and biases they could still reveal much to the historian about the nature and conditions of enslavement in the American South.

Edward E. Baptist adds to this defense of the narratives with an interesting
and extremely insightful argument, which suggests that the stories told in the
interviews between the formerly enslaved and the WPA project workers had been
crafted long before the 1930s. Baptist argues that "identical elements, tropes,
figures of speech, embedded interpretations, and anecdotes appeared in interviews conducted in both the most unpromising and promising conditions." The
repetition of particular narrative techniques suggests that "the stories have been
shaped and spread around the South long before the 1930s and had been etched
into the circuit of individual storyteller's minds long before elderly ex-slaves'
powers of recollection started to fade."[60] Although the WPA narratives cannot
be understood as pure sources and were undoubtedly transformed in the process of telling and retelling, they should be understood as part of a collective vernacular history, "showing who a people thought they were and how they got to
be that way. . . compose[d] . . . of their own rough earth and crooked timbers,
their own everyday metaphors and experiences."[61]

The WPA narratives typically relate the life stories of men and women who
were emancipated. They reflect the experiences of those contemporaneously enslaved men and women rather than runaways or freed people. The narratives
contained in this collection may be considered not as "extraordinary" but as personal and intimate accounts. These narratives reflect the dynamics and daily experiences of enslaved life rather than dramatic stories of escape, challenge, and

freedom. Yet, the WPA narratives are "exceptional" in that they illustrate the ways in which enslaved men and women continued to live in the face of a system which attempted to deny their very personhood.

In fact, Edward Baptist raises a useful point when discussing the WPA collection in relation to longer published narratives of the formerly enslaved, such as those written by Harriet Jacobs and Frederick Douglass two generations before the WPA narratives. These published narratives did, however, employ certain terms and ways of thinking about things that were reiterated in the WPA interviews. Baptist rightly argues that most of the formerly enslaved across the Depression-era South, most of them illiterate and poor, were probably not that familiar with abolitionist literature and therefore could not have been versed in the critiques of slavery featured in these texts. The critiques of slavery found in the 1930s interviews must have come from somewhere, however, and he argues that those who mastered the pen and were able to publish their critiques of slavery, such as Douglass and Jacobs, were "in fact steeped in the same culture of enslaved people that the interviews, in modified form, reveal. By the time [these African American writers] were growing up, their culture had already produced its vernacular history of slavery and forced migration, which eventually surfaced in the 1930s interviews."[62] The collective histories of enslavement were provided with a public platform through these published works; however, the critiques of slavery expressed within them came from a vernacular tradition deriving from the quarters of the enslaved throughout the South.

This book's focus is thematic, exploring the numerous factors shaping the ways in which enslaved men and women managed their romances from within the system of slavery. In chapter 1 I examine the historical construction of identity for the slave and the stereotypical assumptions underlining the slaveholding classes' perceptions of their human property. Stereotypes relating to the sexual licentiousness of slave men and women competed with representations of them as childlike and in need of guidance. The images of "Buck" and "Jezebel" were used by slaveholders to suggest that slave men and women were not capable of experiencing deep emotional feelings, such as love, and that they formed sexual relationships with each other that were casual, fragmentary, and promiscuous. Indeed, the assumed sexual licentiousness of slave women, as portrayed in the image of "Jezebel," was subsequently used to excuse the rape and sexual exploitation enslaved women suffered at the hands of white men.

Conversely, however, slave men and women were also depicted as asexual. Subservient and obsequious, "Mammy" and "Sambo" were the ideal slaves in the eyes of slaveholders. Mammy served her master and mistress faithfully and was also deemed capable of giving and receiving love, although only in the context of her relationship with the planter family and certainly not in the quarters of the enslaved. Slaveholders defined slaves as infantile in nature and relied upon the stereotype of Sambo as evidence that the African race was in need of the slaveholders' guidance and teaching. It was argued that slavery was needed in the South to try and impart certain moral values to slaves and in order to teach them what it meant to be civilized.

These stereotypical images, however, all shared an underlying assumption: that slaves were incapable of falling in love, having romantic attachments or intimate needs and desires. Slaveholders and statesmen such as Thomas Jefferson, as well as visitors to the United States such as Alexis de Tocqueville expressed this view. These arguments were current among the majority of slaveholders and were increasingly used in their justifications for maintaining the institution.

Chapter 2 focuses upon the external forms of influence that interacted in the courtships and romantic relationships of the enslaved. The slaveholder was pivotal to the making of these relationships. Enslaved couples could be sold away from each other without warning on the whim of the slaveholder, whose main concern was profit. Many would never even have had the chance to say goodbye. Parting under these circumstances was sometimes too much to bear. Slaveholders also shaped the form that these relationships took. They had the power to stipulate with whom their slaves could and could not form romantic attachments. Several specified that slaves must court on the home plantation, for example, rather than having relationships that crossed plantations.

For the enslaved on larger plantations or in an urban context slaveholding rules that specified courting on the home place may have proved much easier to achieve than for those living on small farms isolated from contact with the wider community of the enslaved, or those men enslaved in the turpentine camps located at a distance from the home plantation. In addition, the regulation of the working day for the enslaved in North Carolina meant that very often the slaveholder could claim the rights to determine their off-time as much as the time they were expected to labor. The layers of consent that enslaved couples had to peel away were complex and multifarious. Not only were they expected to gain permission from their slaveholders in order to court but also on occasion from the parents of the enslaved woman in question. If one or both of her parents lived close enough, enslaved men were required to prove themselves worthy. Factors such as their owners, their future prospects, and their standing in the quarters and wider community of the enslaved were all concerns of parents when a man sought to court their daughter.

The enslaved learned lessons of morality from their parents, evidenced by the blueprints they carried into freedom relating to issues surrounding courtship, sexual relationships, and marriage. Nevertheless, the Protestant Church also tried to impose moral frameworks upon the enslaved, most clearly evidenced in the records pertaining to church discipline and the enslaved during this period. Many were excluded from their church for "crimes" of a sexual nature— fornication, adultery, and abortion. As I argue in chapter 2, these attempts at regulation by the Protestant church suggests the ways in which it attempted to impose its moral authority upon the enslaved and the ways in which enslaved men and women resisted it.

Courtship was a community event as much as it was a relationship between two people, and in chapter 2 I also highlight the fact that the couple in question was required to gain the approval and support of friends and acquaintances within the enslaved community. Conflict and jealousy are inevitable in any community, however, when it comes to affairs of the heart. The enslaved employed techniques of competition and contest to show off their capabilities to admirers. They also employed methods of conjuration that had been adapted within the context of enslavement from their West African origins. The enslaved made use of various charms and methods of conjure as a means to ward off their competitors and to win the heart of their intended.

The following three chapters then explore how the enslaved responded to these various forms of influence upon their courtships and how they managed to negotiate their own zones of emotional intimacy. In chapter 3 I examine the social and temporal spaces in which courtship could occur for the enslaved. Work and courtship were oftentimes mutually entwined in the lives of the enslaved, and they were often required to adapt the context of their work to allow them to pursue a particular romantic attachment. This situation was especially so in the "authorized" public spaces of events such as corn shuckings and candy pullings or sanctioned holiday periods such as Christmas and layby time. Organized or granted by the slaveholder and therefore remaining under their "gaze," the enslaved adapted these events to invest them with meanings that were completely of their own making. They worked strenuously to inscribe their own mark upon these occasions, and this is most explicitly illustrated in the John Kooner parades that were staged by the enslaved over the Christmas period.

The temporal and social spaces of the church also served as a significant arena in which the enslaved could adapt the meaning of events, such as Sunday meetings, in order to further the limits of their social world. Enslaved couples used the temporal and social spaces of the church in which to court. Moreover, opportunities were presented to ambitious would-be-romancers within the enslaved community through the rules and regulations that demanded that enslaved people sat in a separate section of the church, barred off and separated from members of the white congregation. The prospects this separation raised for a degree of quasi-independent communication between enslaved couples or those seeking a romance were great: the chance to grab a few stolen moments with a lover before entering church, the non-verbal communication of silent gestures that meant so much, and the playful flirtatious manner of some after the enslaved congregation exited the church, through a different door than the whites used.

In chapter 3 I then contrast these authorized social spaces with those of a more illicit and secretive nature: those spaces that the enslaved stole back for themselves. These spaces transcended the defined boundaries of plantation space and the uses to which it might be put. These illicit social events may have been staged on the actual plantation, but they took place in spaces which the enslaved defined as their own. They also took place beyond the plantation on the wider landscapes of enslaved life. Often without the required pass to show the patrollers who made the rounds of local areas in search of errant slaves, enslaved men and women would steal away from the plantation to establish or pursue romantic relationships of their own choosing.[63] The threats presented by the patrol gangs, as well as the dangers posed in traversing the local terrains, meant that the enslaved often had to risk a great deal to see their loved ones.

In chapter 4 I build upon this theme of the subversive practices associated with courtship and argue that enslaved courting relationships should be understood within a broader narrative of resistance. Through their pursuit of a romance they were actively engaged in resisting the system of slavery and their status as slaves. The desire to maintain or establish a courtship forced the enslaved to risk grave physical dangers in the form of the punishments meted out by the patrol gangs and the wrath of the slaveholder. Furthermore, within their romances the enslaved were able to embody particular gendered identities that were denied to them in their status as slaves. This was particularly so for enslaved men who were able to reclaim the identities of provider and protector within the context of these relationships. Thus the places and spaces within which courtship occurred created landscapes upon which the enslaved could engage in everyday forms of resistance that rejected and redefined the modes of control and regulation that attempted to shape the nature of their romantic attachments.

In chapter 5 I explore how the enslaved sought to reclaim their courtship experiences as their own emotional property. This is primarily illustrated through a focus on the wedding days of the enslaved—the climax of courtship. By stressing the aspects of the occasion that were significant to the enslaved themselves, we see that they were involved in an active process of recovering and restructuring understandings of their emotional worlds. The roles of bride and groom were central features of these occasions, allowing the enslaved to step outside their status as slaves and embrace an alternative identity. The ceremony itself was pivotal for enslaved couples who were presented with this opportunity. Performing their ceremony on a public stage provided these couples with a sense of authenticity, which many felt was sorely lacking in the more usual rituals performed by the master and mistress during the wedding ceremony. African American preachers and community sanction played a symbolic and significant role for the enslaved as they sought to validate these unions within the public arena.

Within the collective memories of enslavement couples who were involved in romantic relationships with each other were a testament to how, in spite of the rigors of a system that consistently abused their sense of personhood, they had managed to retain their dignity. Even within a system which contested their rights to emotional autonomy, they had refused to surrender their emotional lives and continued to love and to be loved in spite of the horrors they endured. Even within contemporary literature concerning the enslaved experience they are still being denied their rights to emotional autonomy. The enslaved experience of loving one another—of how they fell in love, managed to court, and reclaimed these intimate moments for themselves—have rarely if ever been apparent. The enslaved, however, did not simply unfold the white flag, signaling their surrender to the degradation and inhumanities of the slave system. They did not just "lie back and think of the good old U.S. of A." Instead, they led complex lives, loving and being loved, in spite of a system that sought to cast them in the role of emotionless, unfeeling, and often violent, black slave.

1

"Love Seems with Them More to be an Eager Desire"

Racialized Stereotypes in the Slaveholding South

THE INTERACTION OF particular views and arguments concerning sexuality and race has been central to discussions concerning the enslaved since the colonial period. The enslaved body and enslaved men and women's sexual identities were constructed in the imaginations of Europeans as symbolic of the "dark continent" of Africa and all that it embodied. The travel accounts of sixteenth- and seventeenth-century male travelers to the Americas and Africa contributed to an emerging stereotype of the nature of West Africans and a view of blackness per se. As historian Jennifer Morgan argues, the African woman and her Native American counterpart became the central figures in racialized stereotypes that created and defined the borders of European national identities and white superiority. She has suggested that, "through the rubric of monstrously 'raced' Amerindian and African women, Europeans found a means to articulate shaping perceptions of themselves as religiously, culturally and phenotypically superior to those black or brown persons they sought to define."[1]

In 1646, the English writer Thomas Browne suggested that "blackness and beauty were mutually dependent, each relying on the other as antithetical proof of each one's existence."[2] The black female figure was continually contrasted to that which was white and therefore considered superior and beautiful. In the travel accounts of European men, African women were defined through and by their sexual identity, which was simultaneously represented as desirable yet grotesque. European observers pointed to what they perceived as African women's alleged capacity for easy childbirth and breastfeeding. This perception would increase in significance over time as it fitted her effortlessly for productive and reproductive labor in the context of New World slavery.

Black women's breasts in particular came to signify their natural propensity for reproduction and childrearing. Richard Ligon, the Royalist refuge, who traveled to the English colony of Barbados in 1647, observed of the West African slave women on the island that "[t]he young Maids have ordinarily very large breasts, which stand strutting out so hard and firm, as no leaping, jumping, or stirring, will cause them to shake any more, than the brawns of their arms. But when they come to be old, and have had five or six children, their breasts hang down below their Navels, so that when they stoop at the common work of weeding, they hang almost to the ground, that at a distance you would think they had six legs."[3]

The links between animality, savagery, and West African sexuality are obvious in the images Ligon has created here. By stressing the robust features of young West African women he reveals that he views them as ideally suited to physical labor in the New World. In addition, he also focuses on their reproductive qualities, noting that they *had five or six children,* a quality that would also be of service in repopulating slave populations. Ligon was quick to add, though, that once female slaves were past the age of reproduction their use was limited, and he depicted them as a grotesque and deformed version of femininity: *At a distance you would think they had six legs.* West African slave women were then characterized as animal-like in form and ideally suited to the task of physical labor and reproduction.

Along with this belief in their heightened fecundity, slave women were also seen to possess a rampant and corrupt sexual appetite. European men had long looked to sexual practices in Africa as being indicative of the corruption and savagery of the black race. English travel writer John Mandeville wrote that in Africa "the folk lie all naked . . . and the women have no shame of the men . . . they wed there no wives, for all the women there be common."[4] By the eighteenth century it was a common assumption made by travelers to Africa and plantation owners in the West Indies that the black woman represented the "sunkissed embodiment of ardency."[5] An English poem published in 1777 concerning the West Indian Island of Jamaica signified such beliefs:

Next comes a warmer race, from sable sprung,
To love each thought, to lust each nerve is strung:
The Samboe dark, and the Mullattoe brown,
The Mestize fair, the well-limb'd Quaderoon,
And jetty Afric, from no spurious sire.
Warm as her soil, and as her sun-on fire.
These sooty dames, well vers'd in Venus' school,
Make love an art, and boast they kiss by rule.[6]

Hence, the black woman's sexuality was defined as simultaneously uncivilized and immoral, yet, to European males, desirable and available. Slaveholding men in the American South would subsequently use images of the "black Jezebel" in order to justify their sexual abuse and exploitation of enslaved women.[7] Her alleged promiscuity and sexual licentiousness were blamed for the seduction of the white man's passions. Moreover, the sexual purity of elite white women was preserved and maintained through the sexual exploitation of the enslaved black woman.

As slavery developed on the North American mainland, racialized stereotypes that were imbued with notions about gender and sexual differences circu-
lated to mark off white society from the enslaved black population.[8] As bearers
of future generations, white women came to embody all that was pure and pious
about the white race. By the early nineteenth century, notions of white womanhood served to bolster the system of slavery as white female purity was contrasted to the alleged sexual depravity of the black female slave. Barbara Welter
argues that the "attributes of true womanhood [were] divided into four cardinal
virtues, piety, purity, submissiveness and domesticity, put them all together and
they spelled mother, daughter, sister, wife—woman." The most essential of these
ingredients was that of purity: "without it she was in fact, no woman at all, but
a member of some lower order."[9]

It was within this lower order that the white southerners located the enslaved woman. She was defined as possessing an active and overt sexuality, which
was contrasted to that of the supposedly chaste elite white woman. The enslaved
woman was cast as the exact opposite of her white mistress in terms of sexual purity and fidelity. This image was given credence through the white man's sexual
exploitation of her.[10] He justified his own actions by shifting the burden of
blame to the enslaved woman and her alleged sexual licentiousness. The paradox
of the contrasting images of elite white and enslaved black women was that white
men used the slave woman's constructed sexual identity in order to establish and
maintain the purity and honor of elite white women. The identity of the enslaved
woman was inextricably bound to the idealized representations of white womanhood, even though she was defined as the antithesis of these images.

In her autobiography Harriet Jacobs described her master's sexual advances
upon her at the age of fifteen. "I now entered on my fifteenth year—a sad ep-
och in the life of a slave girl. My master began to whisper foul words in my ears,
young as I was, I could not remain ignorant of their import." In comparing the
life of the white mistress and that of the slave, she illustrated how black and
white women were defined against each other, one as the idealized image of purity and the other as the embodiment of sin. "The fair child grew up to be a still
fairer woman from childhood to womanhood her pathway was blooming with
flowers and overhead by a sunny sky. . . . How had these years dealt with her slave
sister. . . . She also, was very beautiful; but the flowers and sunshine of love were
not for her. She drank the cup of sin, and shame, and misery whereof her perse-
cuted race are compelled to drink."[11]

The image of the sexualized black Jezebel was a recurrent figure in the
self-serving justifications of enslavement advocated during the late eighteenth
and first half of the nineteenth century. Slave women were then defined as the
epitome of an uncivilized and lewd sexuality. Jezebel was portrayed as a woman
"isolated from the men of her own community . . . liv[ing] free of the social con-
straints that surrounded the sexuality of white women."[12]

The image of Jezebel was primarily used to legitimize the sexual violation of enslaved women at the hands of white men in the slaveholding South. Yet, it also spoke about white fears of black female sexuality. Deborah Gray White has argued that as a stereotype "Jezebel emasculate[d] men by annulling their ability to resist her temptations, and thus her manipulations."[13] The stereotype of Mammy was used to neutralize these fears. Thomas Macon recalled the Mammy on the plantation in Hanover County, Virginia, as his surrogate mother. She was "truly faithful and proud of their control of the little young masters and mistresses, thus relieving their 'old mistresses' of all care in rearing them."[14] In his memoirs concerning life in Virginia before the Civil War Thomas Nelson Page wrote of Mammy as "the zealous, faithful, and efficient assistant of the mistress in all that pertained to the care and training of the children. . . . Her influence was always good. She received, as she gave an unqualified affection."[15] Mammy was thus defined as an affectionate and loyal servant to the white slaveholding classes. To have had located her in the slave quarters where she would have given her affection and love to her husband and her own children would have been unthinkable for these slaveholders.

Because Mammy was defined as asexual in the memories of the slaveholding elite she could therefore be portrayed as the antithesis of Jezebel. Rebecca Latimer Felton recalled her mammy as "a *childless* black woman" who, having been bereft of a child of her own, gave her maternal love to her white charges. "I can see in memory a little child intent on learning things Mammy could teach her, to knit, to sew, to card cotton rolls, and trying to do what Mammy did. I never heard an ugly word from her lips. I never heard my parents utter a cross word to her."[16] Although the image of Jezebel could ease the conscience of slaveholding men, Mammy served to neutralize their fears regarding black female sexuality. Thus, as Deborah Gray White points out, "Together Jezebel and Mammy did a lot of explaining and soothed many a troubled conscience."[17]

Enslaved men too faced a catalogue of assertions regarding their sexual nature and gender identity. Enslavement in the New World presented an affront to the established gender norms of West African society and served to undermine the West African man's sense of masculinity. Male identity in West Africa rested on activities such as hunting and fulfilling the role of the warrior. Consequently, the majority of those enslaved in the West African slave system were women, primarily because in the West African gender order it was women who performed labor intensive and low status tasks such as field work. As Hilary Beckles argues in the context of West African slavery and society, "[i]mportantly, women were expected to perform agricultural labor which was prescribed and understood within the dominant gendered division of labor as 'woman work.'"[18]

The labor regimes on the plantations of the West Indies and the North America mainland represented something that was altogether unfamiliar to West African men. White men did not share a gender ideology that equated agricultural labor with women's work, and West African men were put to work in the fields, performing a variety of labor intensive agricultural tasks. These labor regimes challenged and in many ways undermined the masculine identity of West African men. As Beckles points out, in the context of the early Caribbean slave system, West African gender attitudes and identities were exploded and reconfigured by a system that confronted, rejected, and restructured such ideals.[19] Upon the North American mainland, for enslaved men who were imported directly from West Africa, the labor demanded of them violated West African understandings of appropriate gender divisions of labor.[20]

By the antebellum period enslaved men had regained some authority in the context of work. They had managed to gain a monopoly over more prestigious roles in the labor hierarchy of the enslaved, such as that of the skilled artisan or the slave driver, and were therefore able to reassert a sense of masculine authority within the enslaved community. Moreover, although both men and women performed field labor, they often perceived such activities as "man's work."

Because slaves in North Carolina usually worked under the gang labor system, from sunup to sundown, enslaved women were further defined as distinct from white women through the hard physical work they performed in the field.[21] The work regimes on many plantations and farms therefore often blurred the gender divisions between enslaved men and women. Some enslaved women worked at the same or similar jobs to that of enslaved men in the fields. Lucy Murphy's grandson, John Bectom, recalled that Lucy would get up and "begin burning logs in new grounds before daybreak. They also made her plow, the same as any of the men on the plantation."[22] Clara Jones, who was enslaved in Wake County, also considered the work she performed on Felton McGee's plantation as man's work. She claimed, "I worked lak a man dar an' de hours wus from sunup till dark mostly."[23] Essex Henry remembered that the work on Jake Mordecai's plantation was hard, stating that "I knows case I'se seed my little mammy dig ditches wid de best of 'em. I'se her split 350 rails a day many's de time."[24]

The very fact that these recollections refer to such work as *manly* is indicative that the labor regimes of the plantation often disrupted and offended the gendered norms that existed in the quarters of the enslaved.[25] The work regimes of slaves thus served to enhance definitions of them in wholly physical terms. These particular definitions of labor as "manly" also suggested that a creolized version of gendered identities had emerged among the enslaved by this time, based upon their responses to the circumstances of slavery, the enduring heritage of their West African past, and their interactions with various white cultural values and norms.[26] There had been a significant shift in enslaved conceptions of gender roles, relations, and identities by the early nineteenth century, and the work regimes that were imposed upon the enslaved in antebellum North Carolina offended these gender codes.

The southern slave system attempted to further undermine enslaved men's gender identity by negating their authority in the context of the family and the household. Originating in colonial legislation, any child born to a slave would inherit its mother's status.[27] The role of the father was at once diluted, at least in the eyes of the slaveholder. Furthermore, it was the master and not the enslaved man, as husband or father, who presided over the organization and social relations of the slave family. As Margaret Burnham points out, slave children were technically the equals of their parents at birth. "The slave mother and father could not shape their child's existence, nor could they exercise control over their child's fate."[28] Although the bond between a slave mother and child was largely recognized by the slaveholding classes, they declared the role of the slave father in the life of his children to be invalid.

Deborah Gray White argues that the ultimate control of the slaveholder over both the children and the spouse of enslaved men was an assault on their sense of manhood.[29] Harriet Jacobs related a story in her narrative, which serves to illustrate the profound questions of authority and domination in the lives of enslaved men. She recalled that her brother, William, had been called at the same time by both his father and his mistress; "he hesitated between the two; being perplexed to know which had the strongest claim upon his obedience. He finally concluded to go to his mistress." William's father reproved him for his decision and instructed him, "You are *my* child . . . and when I call you, you should come immediately, if you have to pass through fire and water."[30] Despite the claims of William's father, that William was *his* child, William's behavior demonstrated that it was not the father who commanded the enslaved child's time and governed their behavior but the demands of the master and mistress.

Similarly, in the context of conjugal relationships, enslaved men were forced to witness the physical and sexual abuse of their wives and girlfriends by slaveholders and overseers. White cites examples such as the enslaved man Louis Hughes, who "stood stark still, blood boiling as his master choked his wife for talking back to the mistress. His wife was subsequently tied to a joist in a barn and beaten while he stood powerless to do anything for her."[31] In a slaveholding society such as the American South, where male authority and power was displayed in the context of the household, masculinity could not be disentangled from the ability to protect one's family. Yet slave men such as Louis Hughes, deprived of this power, could only stand by and watch helplessly as the slaveholder physically abused their loved ones. To have intervened in the punishment of his wife was to risk retribution himself. As I argue in chapter 4, enslaved men did sometimes risk their lives to protect their loved ones and in doing so were able to assert a protective masculinity. However, the very fact that enslaved women were threatened with such punishments suggests that the masculine role of enslaved men as protectors of their family was consistently and constantly abused in the slaveholding South.

Stereotypes which stressed the infantile and childlike behavior of enslaved men ostensibly robbed them of any sexual identity during the first half of the nineteenth century. John Blassingame characterizes this image of enslaved men as Sambo, a clownish and congenitally docile slave whose personality traits helped to negate the fear white slaveholders had of their laboring black masses.[32] The image of Sambo is well illustrated in the letters written between members of the slaveholding classes, where they ridiculed the problematic nature of their human chattel and suggested that the system of slavery could serve to benefit the slave man.

Writing to his mother in 1859, Henry Burgwyn presented an image of his slave Dempse that embodied the notions of stupidity and brutish behavior that white southerners used to justify their enslavement of the black race. "You may talk about the trials you have had with 'wide mouth' 'gaping' Edmund but I am sure if you could at this moment step into my room & see the Ethiopian who is honored by waiting on me you would acknowledge Edmund to be a perfect Ganemede when compared to this Fhyestian 'Dempse.'" Dempse is further characterized as the comical and docile servant whom Henry Burgwyn takes much delight in mocking. "His chosen manner of walking is to move with the back bent and with his slim legs curved like a bent bow. When in my presence when he wishes to be particularly graceful & quiet he slides along on tip toe & usually takes steps a yard long. I sometimes see him from my window sailing along as described above at the rate of two forty on the plank."[33]

Henry Burgwyn's images of Dempse and Edmund provide an illustration of the ways in which the slaveholding classes defined slave men as childlike and immature, demanding supervision and guidance from their white masters. The Sambo image offered a specific representation of the slave man, which was projected by the white slaveholding classes and later located in the early historiography of slavery.[34] This was but one white image of black masculinity in the American South, and its intention was to neutralize white fears regarding black male sexuality and assure the white man that in no way was his own power and mastery under threat.

Themes of West African inferiority and dependency were therefore used to underpin arguments that justified and rationalized the system of slavery in the American South. Slaves were defined not only as brutish and savage but also as infantile and in need of guidance from the white slaveholding classes. The system of slavery was justified on the basis that the West African slave and subsequent generations born in the Americas were incapable of caring for themselves and surviving without the guiding hand of their white master and mistress. It was explained thus by Francis Cope Yarnell in his *Letters on Slavery* written in 1853: Slaves "are like children needing constant protection and oversight."[35] Slave men and women were not defined as having an independent or autonomous self, and throughout the centuries of enslavement they were located in the understandings of white southerners as an appendage of their master's plantation and the antithesis of white civility.

Enslaved men were forced to reevaluate their gender identity in the context of the slaveholding South, and they were also simultaneously defined in the popular white imagination as illustrative of an aggressive and dangerous type of masculinity—the racialized stereotype of Buck.[36] It was understood as such in a letter written by Anna Bingham to her daughter, Mary Lynch, in 1839. Anna, who was inquiring about the welfare of one of the slaves who was pregnant on the family's plantation in Orange County, wrote, "I am very anxious to know how Charlotte is by this time. If she has a child I trust it may not have the same father as Clarissa's. I know the shocking depravity of London would give you and Mr. Lynch many uneasy moments. I don't know how you can keep them on the same plantation."[37] The sexuality of slave men was simultaneously defined as rampant and dangerous, especially to the elite white woman of the South, who were represented as the particular object of the black man's sexual urges. Martha Hodes questions whether the black man was characterized as particularly sexually threatening in the context of the slave South. She argues that the image of the sexually menacing black man did not become a prominent issue in the southern white mind until after emancipation when he was no longer subject to the controls of slavery that had maintained his powerless position. Ideas concerning slave men as sexually aggressive are, Hodes suggests, historically inaccurate and represent a projection backward from post-emancipation concerns. Diane Sommerville has also questioned whether southern society was obsessed with the sexual dangers posed by black men during slavery. Sommerville used rape cases involving free and enslaved black men from antebellum Virginia to illustrate the fact that in nearly half of these cases, the accused escaped execution, even after conviction. She subsequently argues that the sexual and racial angst that stimulated the lynch mobs after the Civil War failed to appear before emancipation. The perpetuation of the "rape myth" in the Old South was, in her view, an example of postbellum white angst read backward into the antebellum period.[38]

Such critiques provide new insight into the complex and contradictory images presented of the black man in the antebellum South, most especially in relation to his sexual identity. The very fact that in Virginia from 1800 to 1865, more than 150 black men were condemned to die for sexually assaulting white women and children indicates that the sexuality of the black man was a prevalent concern in antebellum white society.[39] What differed, however, between the antebellum and postbellum periods were the ways in which this perceived threat was managed. In the antebellum period, more than half of those men condemned to die for the crime of rape in Virginia escaped execution, yet it is possible that if they were slaves they received alternative punishments, such as being sold out of Virginia. The sale of a slave man ensured that the slaveholder was financially compensated for the loss of his laborer, but the state was not required to provide this economic remuneration. Thus it was not that the black man was not deemed sexually dangerous during the antebellum period but rather that the slave system shaped the nature of punishment and control. During the postbellum period, white southerners could no longer rely on such mechanisms, and thus they resorted to brutal violence in order to control the perceived threat of the black man and his alleged unbridled and dangerous sexuality.

The slave man occupied a complex and often contradictory position then. While his masculinity was undermined and he was subject to the authority and control of white men, he was also seen to embody an aggressive and threatening sexual nature, which emphasized his masculine identity. Proponents of the slave system could not dispose of a notion that represented slave men as being controlled by physical urges rather than emotional and rational feeling, for this was a fundamental justification employed by white southerners in defense of the slave system. Yet, by advocating the notion of an aggressive black male sexuality, white slaveholders acknowledged that they were not in all ways masterful.

Although representations of slaves as childlike seemed to compete with images that accentuated their sexuality, there was a point of commonality in all these stereotypes. Whether they were cast as being governed wholly by their sexual desires or as childish, immature, and asexual, slave men and women were depicted as incapable of experiencing and expressing emotions such as love for one another in the context of a intimate relationship. They were seen to be governed by physical urges alone and were deemed incapable of experiencing the finer emotions of falling in love or establishing emotional bonds.

Writing during the early republican era, Thomas Jefferson, in his *Notes on the State of Virginia* (1787), declared that the black man was "far more ardent after their female; but [that] love seems with them to be more an eager desire, than a tender delicate mixture of sentiment and sensation."[40] Slave men and, by implication, women were thus defined outside of the boundaries of decent, respectable, and moral forms of loving exchange and this type of discourse was promoted throughout the antebellum period. According to Jefferson, physical desire rather than emotional feeling ruled slaves' expressions of love. To recognize and acknowledge that slaves were capable of feelings such as tenderness and intimacy would have undermined justifications for slavery concerning slaves' moral improvement, and hence have rendered them meaningless. In denying the emotive capacity of the slave man and woman, proponents of the slave system were provided with further justification for their cause.

Although Jefferson pointed to the innate biology of slaves to explain such features of their life, other writers of the period blamed the nature of the slave system itself. Alexis de Tocqueville, in his *Democracy in America* (1835), characterized the familial life of the slaves on the plantations of the American South as devoid of any emotional attachments. Writing about their sexual unions he argues, "The Negro has no family: woman is merely the temporary companion of his pleasures." Tocqueville critiqued the institution of slavery as completely destructive of the individual's ability to establish and maintain relationships which were grounded in a cultivated and refined sense of morality and reason. "If he becomes free, independence is often felt by him to be a heavier burden than slavery; for having learned in the course of his life to submit to everything except reason, he is too unacquainted with her dictates to obey them."[41] While he was not suggesting, as was Jefferson, that the "flaw" was inherent in slaves themselves, the effect of Tocqueville's comments amounted to the same thing. Both commentators defined slaves as incapable of feeling the emotion of love or establishing relationships that were founded on the premise of deep emotional and loving attachment.

Nevertheless, the enslaved did pass through all the trials and tribulations associated with courtship, love, and romance during this period. These issues very much revolved around concepts of authority, consent, and guidance; the geographic and temporal spaces within which courtship occurred; competition within the courtship arena; and the gender roles that men and women assumed within the courting relationship. Of course, they differed somewhat in their understandings of terms such as love, courtship, and romance to those of Tocqueville or Jefferson. The way one conceptualizes such intangible and ephemeral terms is dependent upon various social and cultural factors as well as the individuals themselves. Nevertheless, although battling against the odds, the enslaved did find ways to negotiate around the system of slavery, overcoming the various issues in opposition to their unions and establishing their romantic relationships on their own terms.

2

Asking Master Mack to Court
Competing Spheres of Influence

THE EMOTIONAL LIVES of the enslaved were significant terrains upon which slaveholders could exercise their sense of mastery and claims of ownership. As has been widely documented elsewhere, slaveholders used threats of sale and separation from family members as a tool to discipline and punish their slave populations. In the process they manipulated the emotional ties of their slaves and ripped apart the individual stitches that made up the quarters of the enslaved: budding romances, established courtships, long-term unions, husbands, wives, families, and friends.

Sarah Devereux, in a letter to her brother Thomas, manager of her plantation in Halifax County, demonstrated how the slaveholding classes manipulated the fundamental importance of personal ties to the enslaved and how these ties were used in the plantation system of control and regulation. She wrote of Sally, a female slave: "I have pondered much upon Sallys conduct. . . . I told Sally if such should be the case I would sell her and in the very face of my threat . . . but now it is very hard to sell her, and three children, or without them, I am much perplexed and do not know what is my duty." Sarah Devereux decided to devolve this "duty" to her brother, leaving the final decision of Sally's future in his hands. She told him, "[I]f you think it best to make her an example sell her, you spoke of selling some of yours and may include her if you think best."[1] Sarah Devereux's belief that selling Sally would *make an example of her*, underlines the fact that slaveholders used the threat of sale, as well as the fear of being hired out or moving from housework to fieldwork, as a means to regulate the behavior of their entire slave labor force.

Despite the slaveholders' manipulation and thus recognition of the emotional life of their slaves, slaveholders still defined their labor force as property first and foremost. Almost always the needs and interests of the enslaved were bypassed for the sake of the financial interest of the slaveholder. Ben Johnson, who was formerly enslaved to Gilbert Gregg in Orange County, recalled how his brother, Jim, was sold away from him to secure the money to dress the young mistress of the plantation for her wedding day. He remembered that he had sat under a tree and watched as they had sold him away; "I set dar an' I cry an' cry, 'specially when dey puts de chains on him an' carries him off, an' I ain't neber felt so lonesome in my whole life."[2]

The formerly enslaved Moses Grandy recalled how his wife was sold away after they had been married only eight months: "I have never seen or heard of her from that date to this. I loved her as I loved my life."[3] Heart-wrenching tales of lost love litter the collective memories of enslavement in the South. "Mammy says he don't come home. The next night is the same, and the next. From then on, mammy don't see him no more—never find out what happen to my pappy."[4] The limited possibilities of being reunited left many in despair. "I waited an' I watched, but I didn' hear nuffin. . . . I wus 'fraid de paterollers done kotch him, or maybe he done foun' some gal he lak better dan he do me. So I begin to 'quire 'bout him an' foun' dat his marster dine sol' him to a white man what tuck him 'way down yonder to Alabama. . . . I grieved fo' dat nigger so dat my heart wuz heavy in my breas'. I knowed I would never see him no mo."[5] Recollections such as this were all too familiar among the formerly enslaved as slaveholders and traders both sought profit from dealing in a trade of human beings.

Other slaves were given away to their master's children and near relatives as wedding presents or as part of the marriage portion. New Yorker Sarah Hicks Williams believed that her mother-in-law was spiteful toward her because, as a northerner, Sarah brought no slaves to her marriage to southern slaveholder and physician Dr. Benjamin Williams in 1853. She wrote that her mother-in-law would "never forgive Ben for not marrying niggers, never, never, never!"[6] The slave then was considered as a necessary feature to help further the romantic relationships of the white southern elite and the economic fortunes of the southern elite family. The bitter twist of irony lay in the fact that as the sale of the slave facilitated the union of two young white lovers, it might have undermined that of their enslaved counterparts.

The immense fear of being sold was used by slaveholders as a powerful check on the behavior of their slaves. As Charlie Barbour commented, "[W]e w'oud ov been happy 'cept dat we wuz skeered o' bein sold."[7] The seminal work of Herbert Gutman documents the intense pain and often tragic consequences caused by sale and separation on the familial relationships of the enslaved. Michael Tadman's work on the domestic slave trade in the antebellum South suggests that the separation of families among the enslaved was not as great as previously thought. Nevertheless, he argues that for the lower South the risk of separation during the antebellum period was about one third of that experienced by the enslaved from the upper South, in regions such as North Carolina and Virginia, where 20 percent of enslaved marriages were broken by sale.[8] It is evident from the vernacular histories of enslavement that the slaveholders used the emotional attachments of their slaves as a means of discipline and control and that the intimate ties of the enslaved were very often the casualties of such power relations.

This control of the emotional lives of the enslaved extended to stipulations over who they were allowed to court and marry. Issues such as slave courtship and marriage provoked little direct discussion in the pages of the popular press that were current among southern slaveholders during the antebellum period.[9] Nevertheless, these relationships revolved around questions of consent and the mobility of the enslaved; they were part of larger issues concerning the management of a slave labor force. These issues formed a central component of the slaveholders' conception of themselves, which they then projected to others. They not only suggested to other slaveholders within the community their ability to manage their plantations effectively and efficiently but also allowed the slaveholders to cultivate their image as paternalistic masters whose primary concern was the physical and emotional well-being of their slaves.

Slaveholders usually preferred for their slaves to establish courtships upon the home plantation rather than on neighboring ones. A planter, writing under the name of "Southron," a possible pen name, in 1857, argues that in relation to plantation policies concerning the relationships of slaves, "[m]arriage at home, should be encouraged among them. The practice of taking wives abroad, should as much as possible be prevented."[10] This was primarily tied up with issues of controlling slaves' geographic mobility, what one recent scholar labels the "geographies of containment," determining where slaves could and could not go within and around plantation space.[11] Thus, as "Southron" further points out, "It engenders a habit of rambling, which is injurious to the constitution of the negro, besides removing him frequently and at important times in the influence of the domestic police."[12] Another planter writing for the *Southern Agriculturalist* in 1833 related that the question of slaves maintaining relationships outside of the plantation was utterly objectionable. "[A]llowing the men to marry out of the plantation, [gives] them an uncontrollable right to be frequently absent."[13]

In their quest to prevent these absences, slaveholders laid down certain rules and regulations that they thought were effective in putting an end to this practice. One such planter, who held 150 slaves on his plantation in Mississippi, stated as one of his *Rules and Regulations for the Government of a Southern Plantation* that "It shall be the duty of the driver, at such hours of the night as the overseer may designate, to blow his horn and go around and see that every negro is at his proper place, and to report to the overseer any that may be absent." This rule also stipulated that the overseer should also patrol the quarters himself "at some hour between that time and daybreak . . . and see that every negro is where he should be."[14]

This seemed to be a common method across the slaveholding states concerning plantation discipline. For example, a Virginian planter stated in his article concerning plantation management that "A horn will be sounded every night at nine o'clock, after [which] every negro will be required to be at his quarters, and to retire to rest; and that this rule may be strictly enforced, the manager will frequently adapt a regular and unexpected hours of the night visit the quarters and see that all are present, or punish absentees."[15] The *Southern Cultivator* published an essay in June 1849 entitled "Rules of the Plantation." The fifth rule read thus: "The overseer is not to give passes to the negroes without the employer's consent. The families the negroes are allowed to visit will be specified by the employer." Interestingly, these rules also added a stipulation that the slaveholder would specify which slaves were allowed to visit the premises. Any slave who visited the plantation must show themselves to the slaveholder or overseer.[16]

The rules and regulations of plantation discipline recorded in the popular press of the antebellum era provided a yardstick which individual slaveholders no doubt bended to suit themselves. Mark M. Smith, in his analysis concerning the concept of clock time as it developed in the antebellum South, makes the point that on most plantations all time was ultimately that of the master's, including off-time.[17] Certainly, the working lives of the enslaved were regulated by concepts of time that were imposed and enforced by the slaveholder.

Several among the formerly enslaved recalled the sounding of the horn or the ringing of the plantation bell as symbolic of the mastery the slaveholding classes possessed.[18] Abner Jordan's father was the blacksmith and the foreman on Paul Cameron's plantation, Staggeville, in Durham County. Abner recalled that his father, in his role as foreman on the plantation, "blew de horn for de other niggahs to come in from de fiel' at night."[19] Occasionally the horn and the plantation bell would be used on the plantation to signify different times in the slave's laboring hours. Julius Nelson, who was enslaved in Anson County, remembered that "de ho'n blowed fore de light o' de day an' how we got up an' had our breakfast an' when de ho'n blowed at sunrise we went ter de fiel's in a gallop. At dinner time de plantation bell rung and we'd fly fer home."[20]

Yet, the sounding of the horn or the ringing of the plantation bell also controlled the free time of the enslaved. It was not until the day's labor was done or the season's harvest completed that the master granted his slaves some off-time. Thus, Smith argues, "because the actual, absolute ownership of time was nonnegotiable, masters and slaves came to accept and realize that all time on the plantation, whether work or leisure, was ultimately the master's to bestow, manipulate and define."[21] However, in spite of these disciplinary measures, the enslaved did have limited space in which to negotiate, and often enslaved couples were still able to establish their own intimate ties within a restricted sphere of options.

Examples of how the enslaved negotiated their courtships within the limited options available to them can be seen in the ways in which enslaved men were first required to gain permission to marry from both their own master and that of their intended partner. Parker Pool, who was enslaved in Wake County, recalled that during slavery, when a man loved a woman on another plantation "dey asked der master, sometimes de master would ax de other master if dey all agreed all de slave man an' 'oman had ter de Sa'dy night wuz fer him to come over an' dey would go to bed together."[22] The interesting feature of Parker Pool's comments was that although the actual union of an enslaved man and woman was symbolized in a rather informal manner, the couple was still required to gain the consent of both their masters before their relationship could be legitimized.

This requirement was commonplace for the enslaved, and usually they were required to gain the permission of the slaveholder before even approaching the person in question. Laura Bell recollected how her mother, Minerva Jane, had told her about her courtship with Laura's father, Wesley. Wesley was required to gain consent from their master, Mack Strickland, before he could even initiate any discussion of the subject with Minerva Jane herself. "I'se hearn her tell 'bout how he axed Marse Mack iffen he could cou't mammy an atter Marse Mack sez he can he axes her ter marry him."[23]

In Allen Parker's narrative, *Recollections of Slavery Times*, he recalled the process that enslaved men had to go through when they wished to gain permission to marry a woman who was owned by another slaveholder. He would first gain the consent of his own master, and then he would be subjected to severe questioning and a detailed observation by the master of the woman in question. "[I]f the marriage was a desirable one, it would be in his interests to give his consent, for would not all the children that might be born to the couple be his own property?"

The enslaved man would be expected to return the following week, when the slaveholder might have to be cajoled into remembering the request. "Massa Jones told Sam to come in one week, and den Massa Jones tells Sam as how he can marry Sue or not." If he saw it as a good match, the slaveholder usually obliged; "[W]ell Sam I have talked it over with Sue's Mistress and we have concluded to let you marry Sue, and I will have a cabin built down by the quarters and Sue can live there. . . . In due time the cabin would be built and would be considered as the home of Sue, and also of Sam, whenever he could get permission of his master to leave the plantation or whenever he could manage to steal away without leave."[24]

There is a certain sense of ridicule running through Jones's response to Sam and his request. This ridicule is evident in the way Jones feigned ignorance over Sam's original question, despite him having asked only the week before. He subsequently made Sam repeat his request, thus underlining the dynamics of power structuring the conversation and the sense of control that Jones undoubtedly felt—knowing that if he did not give his consent to this relationship then it would have proven very difficult, although not impossible, to maintain. Nevertheless, the slaveholder had certain factors he had to consider—namely increasing the value of his own personal estate through any offspring produced from the union. This example cleverly illustrates the competing and contesting meanings that were embedded in the courtship experience of the enslaved, the layers of consent that Sam had to peel away, and the humiliation he had to endure in the process.

The primary motive of slaveholders in relation to the courtship of their slaves was clearly understood by the enslaved, as Allen Parker's narrative makes clear. Other slave narratives taken from across the former slaveholding states also make this link. Benjamin Russell, formerly enslaved to Rebecca Nance near Chester, South Carolina, recalled that his master and mistress were always concerned about who their slave women were courting: "For instance, they would be driving along and pass a girl walking with a boy. When she came to the house she would be sent for and questioned . . . 'who was that young man? How come you with him? Don't you ever let me see you with that ape again. If you cannot pick a mate better than that I'll do the picking for you.'" Benjamin's explanation for his owners' concern was quite simple: "The girl must breed good strong serviceable children."[25]

Other slaveholders were not so calculating when considering the relationships of their slaves. A prize-winning essay on the treatment and management of slaves expressed concern that marrying a slave who resided on a different plantation to their own was "always likely to lead to difficulties and troubles, and should be avoided as much as possible." This planter stressed the problems inherent in slaves not being able to live together as husband and wife. The consequence of living on separate plantations resulted in not being able to prove "[the] degree of faithfulness, fidelity, and affection, which owners admire," thus making them loathe to separate these particular couples.[26]

Ethelred Philips requested in a letter to his cousin, James Philips, that he be allowed to hire two of his slaves for the year because of their attachment to their families, who were owned by James. Ethelred explained to James, "I send this by Henry whom I sent by Express with Dory to see his wife. They both seem so much attached to their families I could not have refused them this gratification even if it had not been promised. Please hire them for me this year. Dory would have been willing to stay entirely I think but could not as Henry was unwilling."[27] Ethelred Philips seemed then to understand the ties that bound both Henry and Dory to James Philips's plantation, although we should not neglect the financial motivation that would have accrued in his favor here either. Nevertheless, he appeared to impart a degree of benevolence to those he held in bondage and was consequently willing to hire them out for the year so that these ties could be retained. Drawing upon the memories of the enslaved from other southern states, we can see that this benevolence was practiced by particular slaveholders. Mariah Calloway was enslaved in Wilkes County, Georgia, to Jim and Nancy Willis. She explained that "The Willis family did not object to boys and girls courting. There were large trees and often in the evenings boys from other plantations would come over to see the girls on the Willis plantation. They would stand in groups around the trees, laughing and talking."[28]

In other cases, the relationship between the masters of the courting couple was the fundamental factor governing the romantic relationships of the enslaved. Josephine and Jake Perry belonged to two different masters in Wake County, Nat Whittaker and "Master Middleton" respectively. Their courtship initially took place in secret, because "[w]hen gran'father Jake fell in love wid gran'mammy nobody ain't knowed hit, 'case dere marsters am mad at each other an' dey knows dat dere won't be no marryin' twixt de families." Josephine and Jake courted each other under the cover of darkness until Jake's master followed him one night and caught him in Josephine's cabin. He whipped Jake and then turned on Josephine, only to be stopped by Nat Whittaker, who also bought Jake from Middleton on the same night. "De nex' day he thinks ter ax gran'mammy what Jake am a'doin' in her cabin, an' gran'mammy tells him dat she loves him. Marse Nat laugh fit ter kill an' he sez dat dey'll have a big weddin' at de house fer dem."[29]

Despite Nat Whittaker's response to Josephine's declaration of love for Jake, which probably illustrated his incredulity at the idea of his slaves *being in love*, Josephine and Jake's courtship illustrates one of the possibilities that were open to enslaved men and women in cases where their master rejected their choice of partner. In conducting their courtship in secret they were acknowledging their awareness of the need for consent from their respective masters, yet they recognized that had they tried to obtain such approval, their relationship might have been halted. When their affair was finally exposed they risked punishment and the prospect of separation. Neither Jake nor Josephine could have guaranteed that Nat Whittaker would have been willing to buy Jake and salvage their relationship. In the process of falling in love, this couple had consciously taken risks and constantly endangered their relationship in continuing to court.

Moreover, although seeking the consent of the master and mistress was seemingly required, many enslaved couples from across the slaveholding states courted without the master's permission and sometimes in the face of his refusal to consent to their relationship. Henry Bibb recalled in his published autobiographical account that his own master opposed Henry's courtship with Malinda, an enslaved woman from a neighboring plantation, for fear that Henry would start stealing from him in order to support his new family.[30] Nonetheless, Henry Bibb and Malinda continued their courtship and subsequently married. Whether or not the slaveholder gave consent was fundamental to the form that the courtship took between enslaved couples. If permission was denied, these relationships had to end or carry on in secret if the couple wanted to avoid the wrath of the master and mistress.

The role of the slaveholder in maintaining and protecting ties between enslaved couples was often vital in cases where they were separated by some distance, usually because the planter migrated westward. Slaveholders tended to retain ties with their own families and friends in the local area; consequently, the enslaved were dependent on the slaveholder to act as an intermediary between couples. Betty Foreman Chessier, who was born into slavery in 1843 in Raleigh, North Carolina, recalled that her mother and father met when her father's two masters visited from Arkansas. Betty explained that, "They come over from Arkansas to visit my master and my pappy and mammy met and got married, 'though my pappy only seen my mammy in the summer when his masters come to visit our master and dey took him right back again."[31] Enslaved couples who met and fell in love were often forced to overcome obstacles such as separation, stealing back time and space for themselves whenever they could to share private and intimate moments.

Acting as an intermediary between enslaved couples separated by some distance was usually a role that fell to slave mistresses. This reliance emphasizes the ways in which the dependency of the enslaved upon their master and mistress was written into the southern slave system. This dependency was written into the Southern slave system not only through the slaveholders' care of the physical needs of their slaves but also through the mistress' management and maintenance of their personal relationships.

Anna Bingham from North Carolina moved to the Rediman Plantation in Tennessee sometime during the 1830s with her son, Robert, and his wife, Ann. They took many of the slaves from their estate in North Carolina but left behind Anna's daughter, Mary, and her husband, Thomas Lynch, to run the plantation in Hillsborough, Orange County. The steady flow of correspondence between Anna and Ann in Tennessee to Mary reveal much about the role that the mistress occupied in maintaining and supervising the close personal relationships of their slaves. In one such letter Anna wrote that the "black people also send [their love] to you Charlotte and Clarissa [and] . . . to tell Charlotte and Clarissa their mother begs them to remember her parting advice. She requests me to give her love to London and tell him that Ovid walks all about and she wants to hear of him."[32]

These three women functioned as vital links in the relationships between the enslaved on these two separate plantations. They were thus dependent on the benevolence of their mistress to forward their messages and favors. Anna frequently passed messages on, adding in her own thoughts on the relationship in question. For example, in one letter she wrote of Caty, a slave woman, who had been restless since the move to Tennessee. Writing of a change for the better in Caty, Anna asked that Mary talk to Willie, perhaps a lover of Caty, whom she had been forced to leave behind in North Carolina. She wrote, "[D]o tell my dear Willie the poor creature speaks with distress of his not having spoken to her at parting, she says she did enough to make him angry but wants him to forgive her."[33] Certainly mistresses such as Anna did look beyond the image of human chattel when considering their slave's needs. However, her interference and management in the personal relationships of her slaves, which she seemed to consider necessary and worthwhile, further underlined the ways in which slaveholders were implicated in the emotional lives of the enslaved.

In the same way that Anna Bingham attempted to cement the relationship between Caty and Willie, many mistresses took on the role of matchmaker for their slaves, selecting those they deemed suitable partners, usually for their favored female domestics. This process was distinct from that discussed earlier, in cases where the slaveholder simply paired off slave men and women for economic gain. Mistresses concerned themselves with the personal choices of certain slave women, directing and governing their selections of husbands. Although such behavior may be read as a reflection of the close bonds that could develop between mistresses and their domestic slaves, it can also be understood as part of a implicit system of control and domination that operated on numerous levels.

Such a situation was related in the narrative of Aunt Sally. Sally's mistress proposed the idea of marriage to her after Sally had been taken from fieldwork and placed as a domestic in her mistress's house. Her mistress decided that it was time that Sally had a husband and subsequently suggested the idea to her: "Well Sally, you're thirteen years old and I want you to be married. There's a young man over on the plantation who'll make you a good husband." The proposed husband was Abram Williams, a slave from a nearby plantation, who also belonged to Sally's mistress. Sally was quite shocked at the idea of marriage, but after this initial suggestion her mistress lost no time in pressing the subject with her: "[S]he lost no opportunity to speak of him to the simple hearted girl till Sally said, 'pears like I loved him 'fore I ever saw him.' True to her word the mistress sent for him. They were pleased with each other . . . there was no reason for delaying their union."[34]

The pressure Sally's mistress exerted to force Sally and Abram together could be compared to the experiences of many young white women of the antebellum South, who faced well meaning mothers, aunts, and cousins, keen to have a hand in their romantic affairs. However, few young white women would have been forced into a relationship at such a young age, nor would they have been denied a voice in the matter.[35] Yet for Sally and Abram there was little notion of choice in the process of selection. For young southern white women their choice of beaux was usually extended through older female relatives introducing several favored young gentleman to them. For enslaved individuals such as Sally, their options could be severely limited by the actions of their mistress.

This role as matchmaker was an ironic feature in the mistresses' recognition of the emotional life of their slaves. Although mistresses were willing to concede the right of slaves to pursue personal and intimate relationships, they often continued to direct the nature of such affairs. The shape and course of these courtships was dependent upon the thoughts and actions of the slave mistress. In a perverse twist to these networks of power, slave mistresses displayed disappointment if the enslaved rejected their choices and pursued their own romances.

This sense of regret and disappointment is related in a letter written by Laura Norwood to her mother and father, Thomas and Louisa Lenoir of Fort Defiance, Caldwell County. In it she relates her concern over Eliza, her house slave, and her suitors. She wrote, "I am very much afraid that poor Elias will have to wear the willow. Eliza has a very (?) suitor—whom report says is gaining ground in her favor, but I don't know whether the case is hopeless yet. I shall be very sorry if it is so for he is not of a very good family and they are all a very weakly sickly set he is brother of Bill, the little boy that came with us from Pa's."[36] In November of the same year Laura wrote to her mother, "I have reason to regret Eliza's trip to Wilkes and also her marriage with Elia, but have time non for particulars— Perhaps it will all work right after a while."[37]

Laura Norwood's opposition to Eliza's marriage might have been grounded in a desire for economic gain and also as a display of her own need to maintain power and authority over her property. Whatever the reason, it is possible to detect an element of personal disappointment in Laura Norwood's words over Eliza's choice of partner. She keenly felt that as one of her own favored slaves, Eliza could have bettered herself had she allowed Laura to help her in the process of selection. Moreover, Laura Norwood's comments revealed her belief that she had a right to interfere in the emotional dynamics of Eliza's life. Eliza, however, managed to reclaim ownership of her emotional life, asserted her right to choose her husband, and thus resisted the myriad tentacles of power that stole into the most intimate aspects of her life.

Slaveholders thus recognized the fundamental significance of personal and familial relationships to their slaves. Consequently they were able to use them as a leverage of power over them and as a means to manipulate their behavior. Mistresses in particular often asserted a right of ownership over this aspect of enslaved life, perhaps because the personal and private world of familial relationships within the world of the southern white elite was understood as part of the private and domesticated sphere controlled and governed by women. Occasionally their interest in the personal affairs of a particular slave evidenced the twisted and peculiar notions of power and possession that structured the relationship between slaveholder and slave. However, in their recognition of the emotional needs of their slaves they implicitly acknowledged the personhood of their human chattel and paradoxically strengthened the basis of resistance for the enslaved against such controls.

Another arena within which white slaveholders could exert a certain degree of social control was through religious worship and within the social context of the church.[38] On the North American mainland, large numbers of the enslaved had embraced their own forms of Protestant Christianity by the antebellum period, melding their West African heritage with the teachings and ideals of the Christian Church. Both biracial Methodist and Baptist churches were growing throughout North Carolina during the first quarter of the nineteenth century, particularly in large towns such as Wilmington, and there were a small but growing number of African American preachers during this period. However, the majority of rural slaves still remained outside the institutional reach of the church at this point.

Demark Vesey's rebellion in Charleston in 1822 and Nat Turner's uprising in 1831, in Southampton County, Virginia, caused a severe backlash against the independent institutions of African American Christians, and they thus saw their limited sense of agency vested in these religious activities severely restrained. Legislation passed in North Carolina in 1831 that focused on the role of the African American preacher suggested such tightening of controls: "Be it enacted by the General Assembly of the State of North Carolina . . . that it shall not be lawful under any pretence for any free negro, slave or free person of color to preach or exhort in public, or in any manner to officiate as a preacher or teacher in any prayer meeting or other association for worship where slaves of different families are collected together." Those who flouted this legislation, slave and free, were to receive no more than "39 lashes on their bare back."[39]

However, by the 1830s slaveholders had largely come to accept the benefits of conversion among their slaves, despite potential and actual insurrections and the revolutionary implications of religious teaching. They began to condone the work of white Protestant missionaries in the South, such as the Presbyterian minister Charles Colcock Jones, who was at the forefront of the plantation mission movement, intended to take the Protestant faith to the slave masses. Morality was an important theme in the religious instruction of slaves, and all three of the main Protestant denominations—Methodist, Baptist, and Presbyterian—attempted to impose their own moral codes on slave men and women. Although high moral standards were already common within the quarters of the enslaved, Protestant denominations still felt it necessary to reinforce certain ideals and impose them on their slave brethren.

In his 13th Annual Report of the Association for the Religious Instruction of Slaves, Jones advised slaveholders on the moral discipline and culture of their slaves. He stressed that the duty of slaveholders was to enforce moral discipline among their slaves, which could be done through fulfilling a number of duties. Slaveholders were advised to "provide sufficient and separate accommodations for the families of their servants . . . not separate[ing], nor allow[ing] the separation of husband and wife, unless for causes lawful before God" and suggesting that they "use every effort to promote morality upon their plantations . . . [and] prohibit quarrelling and fighting and profane swearing." Jones advocates the "suppression of vice and immorality and to the encouragement and protection of piety and virtue."[40]

In his instruction that masters should promote morality on their plantations, Jones suggested several ways in which this might be achieved, focusing in particular on the nature and course of courtship for slaves. He advised slaveholders that "owners should encourage early marriages, and take an interest in seeing that the connections which their people form are suitable and promising in character." Taking a special interest in the morality of young adults and adolescent slaves, he instructed "that they be not allowed to keep late hours: that they be not allowed to visit abroad at will, frequenting corn-huskings or dances; but when they visit abroad let it be under the care of some one of their responsible relations or friends; nor should visitors be allowed to frequent a plantation without making their intentions known."[41] It is clear from these instructions that Jones was concerned with trying to enforce a particular morality upon slaves, something he believed the majority of them were lacking. "[T]hey are in the mass a degraded people in their morality," he writes, urging Christian masters and mistresses to correct the behavior of their charges: "The moral state of the negroes on plantations, depends greatly upon *the character of their owners and interest which they take in restraining vice and encouraging virtue.*"[42]

The regulation of slaves' morality—and indeed that of the wider black community—was a constant theme of all the main Protestant denominations during this period. This preoccupation is well documented through the records of the church disciplinary committees that were formed to hear charges brought against church members for various misdemeanors and conduct that was considered "unchristian." Of course, it should be noted at this point that white as well as slave and free black members of the church had charges brought against them for a number of alleged crimes, such as drunkenness, swearing, and bastardy. Nevertheless, the charges brought against enslaved members of the church are particularly interesting because of the network of power dynamics that they exposed between master, slave, and community within the antebellum South.

For example, at the Grace Methodist Episcopal Church, Wilmington, between the years 1832 and 1852, 49 white members were excommunicated, compared to 389 colored members. Although allowances must be made for the greater number of African Americans than whites in Wilmington during the antebellum period, it is noteworthy that for the period 1846 and 1852, the discrepancy between expulsion rates for white and colored members was .6 percent and 2.7 percent per year respectively. The power and ritual associated with excommunication would have had a huge effect on an individual's standing within the community—be they white or black, slave or free. Yet, the fact the excommunication rates for enslaved individuals stand at a much higher rate than they do for those white individuals hints at the ways in which "church discipline was utilized as a means for maintaining control over the slave population."[43]

Concern over slave morality was sometimes perceived as a problem within the black community as a whole. Hence, at their monthly meeting in April 1822, the Sawyers Creek Baptist Church agreed to appoint a committee to "enquire into the State and standing of the Black Brethren and sisters and report to the white Deacons every quarterly meeting."[44] The moral standards of all the African Americans belonging to the church, enslaved and free, were to be subject to intense scrutiny by their fellow white church members. Individual charges brought against enslaved men and women were also held up as examples to the rest of the enslaved community, much as slaveholders used the sale or the hiring out of slaves as a threat to the rest of their slave laborers. The consequences of such charges for the majority of the enslaved was excommunication, although on occasion individuals could be restored to membership after a considered amount of time, and in a limited number of cases they were acquitted of charges brought against them. For example, Grace, who was an enslaved member of the Wheelers Baptist Church in Person County, was charged with "drinking too much spirits" in April 1848. However, because she "came forward and acknowledged her guilt and confessed Repentance" the church forgave her.[45] Enslaved men and women who were excommunicated from their churches could suffer a considerable deterioration of standing within the enslaved community, and they may have consequently found it more difficult to gain the consent for their courtship from important influences such as the slaveholder, the parents, or the wider community.

The range of activities that resulted in the excommunication of enslaved men and women from Protestant churches was broad. These activities could include moral crimes such as that committed in August 1829 by the enslaved woman Patience, who was charged with dancing by the Hepzibah Baptist Church in Wake County. Alternatively, charges could include theft, such as the case of the enslaved man Wiley, who was excluded from the Red Bank Baptist Church in Pitt County in 1846.[46] Clearly, Protestant ministers negotiated their authority over the enslaved with that of the slaveholder, and charges were brought against the slave for such behavior as disobeying the master, running away, and concealing cotton, which in every case resulted in exclusion from church membership.[47] The complex and multilayered mechanisms of authority in the regulation of slave morality can be seen to interact and reinforce each other at numerous points, and biracial Protestant churches mediated a concern for the spiritual welfare of slaves with an explicit awareness of the rights of ownership slaveholders claimed over their human chattel.

Several of the charges brought against enslaved men and women were those of a sexual nature and thus reinforce the argument that Protestant denominations were particularly keen to impose strict sexual morals on their slave brethren. For example, in the disciplinary committee records of the Hepzibah Baptist Church between 1810 and 1840, twelve black members were excluded on the charge of adultery. The next ranking charge was for theft, for which a significantly smaller number—that of seven—black members were excluded. Aside from charges of adultery there are various cases within the Hepzibah Baptist Church minutes that reflect the authorities' preoccupation with "crimes of a moral nature." For example, the enslaved woman Sadie was excluded for an unmarried pregnancy, in 1833, as was the enslaved woman, Becky, for aborting her child. Interestingly, her mother, who had aided her daughter in this operation, was also excluded.[48]

The minutes of the Sawyers Creek Baptist Church, Camden County, document numerous such cases including that of "Angelica Gregory, a col. Sister the property of Rev. M. R. Gregory," who on June 10, 1857, was expelled on the charge of fornication.[49] She had been among a number of African American women who had been expelled from the church for a variety of sexual misdemeanors. These cases included that of a slave woman named Phillis, who was expelled on the charge of bastardy in 1845, and Tilsey Lamb, "a colored sister," who was expelled for adultery in 1857.[50]

The charges brought against these men and women—from dancing to theft to fornication to abortion—suggest that the enslaved resisted the desire of those of the Protestant faith to impose their own moral frameworks onto their slave members. The enslaved faced numerous complications and problematic issues in their lives, and it was often difficult, if not impossible, to conform to the strict standards imposed by the Protestant Church. The case of Becky, who aborted her unborn baby with the help of her mother, could possibly have been the result of sexual assault by her master or the overseer, thus explaining why she felt unable to have the child. Alternatively, Becky may have felt that her child was better off unborn than being forced to live a life of slavery. Likewise, the enslaved man Wiley, who was charged with theft, may have been taking food to feed his family, supplementing the meager rations of the plantation. Thus, there were a myriad of factors that should be considered when examining these cases primarily because of the intricacies of enslaved life and the competing demands that were made upon them by master, church, and the enslaved community.

Enslaved ideas about appropriate standards of morality were shaped by numerous factors, especially their religious beliefs—Christian and otherwise. They may have chosen to resist the strict moral guidelines laid down by their church. Cases such as Patience, who was expelled from church for dancing, come to mind. Although the enslaved may have chosen to embrace the religion of their slaveholders, they also tried to retain cultural norms within their own communities, constructed from their West African cultural heritage and reshaped within the context of enslavement. This merger produced contradictions in the enslaved experience, and never more than in their relationship to religious practices. Some enslaved men and women chose to embrace the strict teachings of the Protestant church in its entirety. John Jackson claimed that at the church he attended in Wilmington "all our people marched behind our owners, an' sat in the galle'y. Now them that went to St James church . . . were taught they were better then anybody else. That was called the 'silk stockin' church. Nobody else was fittin to look at."[51] Evidently, some enslaved men and women sought to conform to the strict rules that Protestant churches imposed upon them. Yet, it should also be noted that others may well have chosen to resist the teachings of a Protestant religion in favor of a more fluid and forgiving set of principles. This preference wasn't entirely surprising given that the bulk of teachings from white Protestant ministers, as one formerly enslaved woman recalled, mostly taught them to "obey their marsters and missus that the Bible said obey."[52]

The enslaved established their moral framework within numerous locations largely developing their moral standards from the lessons they learned from the enslaved community—African American preachers, parents, and elders—rather than their masters and mistresses or white preachers. The communities of the enslaved were structured by strong moral codes that they were forced to adapt to the conditions and experiences of enslavement. Enslaved mothers and fathers sought to protect their daughters from the sexual overtures of men—enslaved and free, black and white for an extensive period of time stretching beyond adolescence. Of course, this wasn't always possible in the face of sexual exploitation, especially from the overseer and the master, but the fact that enslaved parents persevered in establishing high moral standards for their daughters and, in addition, for their sons, setting examples of the ways in which gender codes of conduct operated and the exact rules of courtship for men and women, should be regarded as extremely significant.

Despite the fact that the slaveholder was the dominant authority figure in the public lives of slaves, and the Protestant Church attempted to impose its own version of morality upon slave communities, in the private worlds of enslaved men and women, gaining the approval of a woman's family was of paramount importance in defining the courtship experiences. Conflict no doubt erupted between enslaved men and women and their parents over their choices concerning who they fell in love with. Rumor and gossip were also virulent within the majority of enslaved communities throughout the South. Hearsay and tittle-tattle over the latest courtship would doubtless have served as an avenue of escape from the daily horrors of the lives that the enslaved were being forced to live. This would without question have acted upon the ways in which enslaved men and women would have presented themselves to the wider enslaved community and would no doubt have made young enslaved men more conscious of demonstrating themselves to their peers, lest any prospective beaux be in the vicinity of the quarter.[53] As Larry Hudson argues, "because of divisions within the slave community, young men wishing to marry a young woman from richer and more powerful slave families would have experienced considerable pressure to display their ability to provide for themselves before they could anticipate any success in winning their heart's desire."[54]

The majority of parents who were living near enough to their daughters to have knowledge of their courtships would have sought to guide them in their choices toward men of good standing within the enslaved community and belonging to a good Christian family rather than "a 'no-account nigger' owned by a failed planter or let out to a poor white."[55] Andy Marion, who had been born into slavery in South Carolina in 1844, recollected that courting somebody was a multifaceted process whereby the enslaved were often required to peel away the layers of consent, which included gaining permission from slaveholders, acceptance of the girl herself, and parental consent: "[D]e gal got to consent, de gal's daddy got to consent, de gal's mammy got to consent. It was a hell of a way."[56] On Dr. Peter Hoyle's plantation in Decatur, Georgia, parental blessing concerning courtship among the enslaved was paramount. According to the formerly enslaved Camilla Jackson, "A young man courted the girl in the presence of the parents . . . when he left, the mother would go to the door with him."[57]

Several formerly enslaved men and women referred to parental influence being exerted on their courtship after freedom during the postbellum period. On the surface, we might infer from this that parental consent only became a significant factor after emancipation as the formerly enslaved gradually regained control and authority over their personal and emotional lives. However, it also suggests that the enslaved carried a strong moral framework into freedom, established and cultivated from within the system of slavery. Parents tended to stress the lessons they had learned from their own courtship experiences concerning broken and mended hearts, maintaining one's respect, and receiving respect in return.

Laura Bell, the daughter of Wesley and Minerva Jane, discussed earlier in this chapter, recalled in her narrative how the lessons that her parents had learned while courting were passed down to Laura and her suitor. Following emancipation Laura met Thomas Bell. However because she was only twelve years old, "[m]y folks said dat I wus too young fer ter keep company so I had to see him 'roun' an' about for seberal years, I think till I was fifteen."[58] Wesley and Minerva Jane's influence in the courtship of their daughter emerged as a response to their own experiences during slavery. They prevented Laura from engaging in any form of intimate relationship until she was of an age that they considered appropriate. Laura's sexual honor was thus protected by her parents, who may have struggled to achieve such ends during their own youth because of the threat of sexual abuse and the sadistic forms of punishment that were often meted out to slaves.

Formerly enslaved men and women attempted to shape and define the courting relationships of their children in the postemancipation period based upon their own experiences during slavery. In turn, children of the formerly enslaved seemed to acknowledge and accept the morals that their parents imparted to them. The acknowledgement and acceptance of parental advice was evidenced by

Laura Bell's reaction to Thomas's advances. Following his proposal of marriage, Laura accepted but she refused to allow Thomas to kiss her, explaining that, "he has ter wait till we gits married."[59]

Although many couples must have despised the power that the slaveholder had over the fate of their romances, formerly enslaved men and women did seek to exert a degree of influence over the courtships of their children in the post-emancipation era. Laura had been instructed by Minerva Jane and Wesley not to court Thomas until they considered her to be of a suitable courting age. Similarly, Lucy Ann Dunn's mother, Rachel, who had been enslaved in Wake County, was the dominant authority figure in Lucy Ann's romance with Jim, which occurred in the immediate aftermath of emancipation. After three Sundays of meeting at the church in Neuse, Jim finally asked if he could walk Lucy Ann home. She recalled, "[w]e walked dat mile home in front of my mammy an' I was so happy dat I ain't thought hit a half a mile home. We et cornbread an' turnips for dinner an' hit was night 'fore he went home. Mammy wouldn't let me walk wid him ter de gate. I knowed so I jist sot dar on de porch an' sez good night."[60] Lucy Ann's mother appeared as the controlling influence upon their relationship from the moment that Jim and Lucy Ann began courting. They were made to walk home in front of her, so she might keep a watchful eye on the young couple. Lucy Ann, aware of her mother's authority, would not even walk Jim to the gate when he left, but remained on the porch to say goodnight.

Following a courtship that lasted a year, Jim proposed to Lucy Ann. Rachel's advice to her daughter on the matter reflected the value that a formerly enslaved woman attached to marriage. Rachel had been the cook on the plantation belonging to Peterson Dunn of Neuse in Wake County before emancipation. She had a husband named Dempsey, who was also enslaved, and she had bore him five children, all born into bondage. Following Jim's proposal, Rachel reminded Lucy Ann "how serious gittin' married is an' dat hit lasts a powerful long time."[61]

For Rachel to have imparted this advice to Lucy Ann illustrates the fundamental significance that the formerly enslaved accorded to the creation of family bonds, particularly through marriage. Contrary to the assertions of white southern slaveholders and the majority of white southerners during the antebellum and postemancipation period, the enslaved emerged into freedom with well-grounded ideas about the importance of institutions such as courtship and marriage, stressing the permanence and strength of these relationships.

Aside from seeking parental consent, enslaved men and women would have sought the acceptance of the wider enslaved community for their relationship. Community acceptance may have proved difficult given the competition and rivalry that would have existed in this arena. The most visible result of jealousy was the competition that could occur between enslaved men and women vying for each other's attentions. Hannah Crasson recalled how her aunt used to display her dancing abilities at the frolics she would attend. "She wuz a royal slave. She could dance all over de place wid a tumbler of water on her head, widout spilling it."[62] Hannah Crasson's aunt was no doubt seeking to impress enslaved men with her dancing skills as well as inviting competition from those enslaved women who dared to challenge her.

This competitiveness could sometimes lead to argument and conflict. Examples taken from across the former slaveholding states indicated how conflict could erupt in the context of courtship. Lucinda Davis, who was interviewed at Tulsa, Oklahoma, remembered that the various kinds of dances performed at frolics of the enslaved would often lead to trouble. "[D]e worst one was de drunk dance. Dey just dance every which-a-way, de men and de women together and dey wrassle and hug and carry on awful." She went on say that this particular "drunk dance" could lead to conflict and domestic violence, especially if the couple dancing slipped out together to the woods. "Dat kind of doing make de good people mad, and sometimes dey have killings about it. When a man catch one of his women—maybeso his wife or one of his daughters—been to de woods, he catch her and beat her and cut off de rim of her ears"[63]

When the formerly enslaved Anderson Bates courted his intended, Carrie, he describes himself as "falling head over heels in love" with her. Carrie, however, had attracted the attentions of numerous men on the plantation and Anderson related how he saw his competitors off. "I knocks one down one night, kick another one de nex' night, and choke de stuffin' out of one de nex' night." Carrie and Anderson had some harsh words about the way he treated these men, but their relationship eventually resulted in marriage.[64]

Certainly slaveholders were not unaware of the conflict that could be generated among their slaves. Fights among slave women were particularly disagreeable to the slaveholder, presumably because this was not how women should behave. One slaveholder writing for *De Bow's Review* was particularly adamant in his advice to the overseer concerning slave women fighting: "Fighting particularly among women, and obscene or abusive language is always to be vigorously punished."[65] Walter W. Lenoir also complained about the task of controlling female slaves. Writing to his mother in 1864 from Crab Orchard in Caldwell or Watauga County, he told her that "I find upon trial so far that I can manage the men and boys with more comfort than I expected; but though I always considered she negroes a pest, mine are dirtier and lazier than I ever counted on." He considered himself to be very much to blame for this state of affairs, however, declaring that "I have not yet attempted to control them." He concluded his letter by vowing that he would "nerve [him]self for the very disagreeable task of instituting and keeping up a strict discipline over them."[66]

Another less visible and furtive means of warding off one's opponents within the arena of courtship was to be found in conjure. Sharla Fett, in her brilliant discussion of health and healing among the enslaved, argues that the

conjuror clearly represented a relational vision of health and healing, which
"connected individual health to broader community relationships." Within this
relational vision of health, the enslaved assumed that conflict would be present
not only in their relationship with slaveholders but also within their community
life. The power of healing could be both good and bad, depending on how it
was harnessed, and the art of conjuration was often used by the enslaved as a tool
against other members of their community in their contests over courtship. As
Fett points out, "Accounts of conjuring reveal that men and women frequently
'worked roots' to resolve or escalate personal disagreements that had little to do
with the immediate actions of whites."[67]

The concept of conjuration as a force in the daily lives of the enslaved and
its uses as a central element within enslaved conflict and competition was recollected by many among the formerly enslaved. Patsy Mitchner remembered that,
although she had never had a spell put on her, she "knowed a woman once who
had a spell put on 'er, en' it hurt her feet."[68] Similarly, Ellen Trell told the story of
her mother, who had a spell put on her: "[S]he lay in bed talking to herself and
sweating drops of sweat as big as the end of my finger."[69] These strong beliefs
in the power of magic and spells made many fearful of any suspected witches.[70]
Thus, Penny Williams slept with a knife under her pillow ever since a witch had
tried to ride her. She explained that "I was in de bed, an' she thought dat I was
'sleep. I feels her when she crawls up on my lef' leg an' stops de circulation. I
knows how ter fix her do' so I gits up an' puts a knife under my pillow."[71] Laura
Sorrell's parents were so frightened of the effects of magic that they paid the
witch doctor "a right smart ter keep off de witches."[72]

The use of conjuration in the arena of courtship was a central element in enslaved practices across the slaveholding South, and signs and symbols were often
used as points of reference and reaction. For example, in his narrative, the formerly enslaved Henry Bibb described how he made use of a conjuror in his efforts to win the attention of a young woman on his plantation. The conjuror
provided Henry with charms such as the bone of a dried frog, and other remedies included Henry obtaining a lock of his intended's hair, which he was then
instructed to wear in his shoes. Henry Bibb found little success in any magical
remedies offered to him.[73] However, what is significant is that his faith in the
use of such charms continued despite their lack of success. Even after the dried
frog bone had scared his intended belle rather than magically captured her heart,
Henry visited another conjuror seeking another love charm. Within the WPA
collection several of the formerly enslaved related conjuration techniques to cap-
ture the heart of your intended. These methods included a woman wearing a
section of the man's cap close to her body "if she wishes to make the man fall
in love with her." It also advised that a man "may also cause a woman to fall in
love with him by letting her drink whisky in which he has allowed 'Gin-root'
to soak."[74]

This resonated strongly within the cultural worlds of the enslaved, where these ideas concerning courtship and notions of conjuration were replicated in their folklore tales. This folklore narrated the realities of life under slavery, and central to their themes were the concepts of competition and contest *within* the enslaved community, particularly over women and food. Thus, within these stories the trickster character often employed "bad magic" to win the hand of his intended.[75] These sources do not provide any consistent or coherent picture about what love was or what it was supposed to represent among the enslaved. However, they do present the idea that love and the processes that one went through in the journey toward capturing one's hearts desire was not just an emotional feature of life but that which manifested itself physically and could be altered through external influences. These forces were not solely those already familiar to the social historian of the slaveholding South—namely, the governance and authority of the slave owner or the destructiveness of the slave system. Instead, they narrated episodes where love fell victim to trickery and deceit, most commonly through practices of conjuration.

The human heart is a fragile organ, susceptible to the slightest pressure or change of circumstance. Within their courtships and romantic affairs the enslaved felt these pressures—insecurity, doubt, fear—not only as a consequence of these relationships within their own private lives, but also as human chattel in the wider systems of power that structured the slaveholding worlds of the antebellum south. Within this world they were required to live a life of uncertainty, surrendering their fate to men and women whose primary objective was profit.

The demands of the labor system that were imposed upon them meant that they were often forced to shape their courting relationships within the physical boundaries of the plantation as an extension of their working day. Certain events that were seemingly associated with work, such as corn shuckings, were in fact used by the enslaved as opportunities to extend the limits of their personal worlds, socialize with members of the opposite sex, and possibly pursue a courtship. Other social contexts also served as ideal opportunities in which to pursue courtships for the enslaved. For example, the social and temporal spaces that attendance at Sunday service provided were a primary means through which enslaved men and women furthered their romantic affairs. Furthermore, the enslaved could also meet at more secret gatherings such as illicit frolics, held in the quarters of the enslaved or at locations beyond the plantation.

Hence, the social and temporal spaces of courtship represented a broad terrain upon which the slaveholder and the enslaved negotiated and contested rights of ownership. As one scholar of slavery points out, "[S]laves and slaveholders did not fight their battles on equal grounds."[76] However, the enslaved were able to confront, contest, and challenge the authority of the slaveholder in the social spaces of courtship, in part, through creating a social world that was both of and apart from, the realities of plantation life.

3

Getting Out to Play and Courting All They Pleased

The Social and Temporal Geographies of Enslaved Courtship

A NNA WRIGHT'S MOTHER had been enslaved to James Ellis in Scotland County. She recalled that during slavery, although "de slaves worked hard in de fiel's . . . unless de work wus pushin' dey had Sadday evening off ter go a-fishin er do anything de wanted ter do." Elaborating upon the ways in which the enslaved spent their leisure time and the slaveholder's role in this, Anna Wright recalled her mother's remembrances:

> Two or three times a year Marse James let dem have a dance an' invite all de neighborhood slaves. Dey had corn shuckin's ever' fall an' de other slaves 'ud come ter dem. De candy pullin's wus a big affair. . . . Dey'd come from all over de neighbourhood ter cook de lasses and pull de candy. While de candy cooked dey'd play drappin de handkerchief an' a heap of other games. De courtin' couples liked dese games 'case dey could get out an play and court all dey pleased.[1]

Anna's comments reveal much about the ways in which the enslaved were able to extend the limits of their social lives, the role of the slaveholder in structuring such experiences, and the opportunities presented on such occasions for them to establish more intimate relationships with members of the opposite sex. However, they also only reveal half the story. Although the enslaved were more than willing to embrace those occasions offered by the slaveholder in which to "get out an play," they also pursued their courtships during time that they stole back from the slaveholder, illustrated in illicit night visits and illegitimate social gatherings occurring away from the gaze of the slaveholders and beyond their governance.

Falling in love and establishing a courting relationship for the enslaved was divided into two competing spaces: authorized free time, which was controlled and regulated by the slaveholder, and that time which the enslaved took back for themselves.[2] Of course, these two social spaces were never completely separate, interacting at numerous different levels and both being subject to the mechanisms and shape of slavery within North Carolina. Yet, attempts made by the enslaved to establish and maintain their courtships in spaces that transcended the temporal and spatial limits imposed upon their lives should be understood as part of a broader narrative of conflict, tension, and subtle contest between slaveholder and slave in the antebellum South.

North Carolina was comprised of distinct and diverse economic districts that were based on the export of specific crops or produce. The work regimes of the enslaved were dictated in each district by the specific demands of these particular goods. These work routines were fundamental to the wider dynamics of enslaved life, and as Ira Berlin and Philip Morgan argued, "the legacy of slavery cannot be understood without a full appreciation of the way in which slaves worked."[3] Slaves were, after all, defined first and foremost in the minds of their white masters and mistresses, and in legal terms, as laborers, and wider aspects of their life, such as courtship and social relationships, were primarily shaped by the dictates of their work regimes.

Many field slaves did not specialize in the cultivation of a single crop but grew and harvested a variety of produce, including corn, wheat, and cotton. They also worked at raising cattle and hogs and maintaining and improving the land. Large plantations not only produced goods for wider markets but also grew and manufactured produce for home consumption.

For example, William Pettigrew, a slaveholder from Washington County, listed his real property in 1860 as including three horses, twenty mules, six milk cows, sixteen working oxen, ten beef cattle, fifty-three sheep, and ninety-six swine. In 1859 his slaves on his plantation, Magnolia, had raised 9,000 bushels of corn, 500 bushels of sweet potatoes, 50,000 pounds of fodder, and 300 bushels of peas. They had also manufactured 150 pounds of butter and 100 yards of cloth from locally grown flax and wool.[4] For slave men and women based on such plantations, labor demands could be multiple and varied. The gang labor system required less specialization in terms of labor skills and ensured that the diverse needs of the plantation system were met. This approach was in contrast to the task system common in the South Carolinian low country, which called for specific skills that were concentrated on a particular task.[5] The major difference between the two labor systems was that gang labor ensured that slaves toiled for as long as possible each day, and in the task system as soon as a slave's allotted tasks were completed any time left in the day was his or her own own to spend on domestic tasks such as cultivating their gardens plots or washing clothes. Enslaved men and women in North Carolina recalled long days in the field and rarely referred to a system that reflected tasking in their work.

Charlie Barbour, enslaved in Johnston County, remarked that his master "wucked his niggers from daylight till dark, an' his thirteen grown slaves had ter ten' 'bout three hundred acres o' land . . . dey mostly planted co'n, peas an' vege'ables."[6] Henry Bobbitt, who had belonged to Richard Bobbitt of Warren County, also reported this type of labor system and diversity of crops in his recollections of enslavement: "We farmed, makin' tobacco, cotton, co'n, wheat an' taters. Massa Dick had a whole passel o' fine horses an' our Sunday job wuz ter take care of 'em, an' clean up round de house. Yes mam, we wucked seben days a week, from sunup till sundown six days, an' from seben till three or four on a Sunday."[7]

Periods of the agricultural season that demanded intense physical labor may have resulted in less time and energy on the part of the enslaved to engage in the pursuit of a courtship. Slave laborers who were not part of plantation or farm life but worked in the growing industries of North Carolina, such as that of turpentine and naval products, generally lived in camps located within the pine forests and were more isolated from the wider community. This was especially so in the eastern counties, which were rich in the long leaf pine used in the production of such materials. The turpentine industry operated on a task system as opposed to the gang labor system used on the plantation. For slaves who worked in the turpentine industry, the year was divided into specific tasks that required immense skill and strength and demanded intensive labor. Jonathan Worth, who owned a turpentine plantation in Wilmington, wrote to his son David Gaston Worth in 1853 after spending ten days on the turpentine plantation. He reported that "I had from 16 to 20 hands and had made about 15 thousand boxes . . . the black hands were making from 2000 to 25000 boxes per day. The prospect is pretty fair for getting 200,000 boxes."[8]

This was hard, unrelenting, manual work which required a good deal of physical strength and stamina. Physically exhausted, the enslaved based on turpentine camps would have found it difficult to muster the energy, both bodily and mentally, to pursue a romance in their off-time. Aside from the constant labor demanded, life on the turpentine plantation was often isolated, detached, and lonely. Although the task system afforded them a relative degree of autonomy, the camps themselves were typically located far away from agricultural plantations and the processing of the turpentine itself. The turpentine industry relied on the physical strength of slave men for the heavy tasks involved in the production of turpentine and thus, men dominated the labor force. Reflecting this gender division of labor among the turpentine workers, *The Southern Cultivator* reported in an article concerning the naval stores industry in 1846 that "the same boxes will stand tending or chipping from eight to ten years, which labor is performed by males, both white and slave, women and children not being very serviceable."[9] Located in the pine forest, isolated from the wider community and more importantly female company, the men enslaved in these camps must have suffered, reliant upon each other's support to see them through the long, exhausting, and often lonely days and nights.

The conditions and experiences of enslavement were extremely varied then depending upon their geographical location, the size of the plantation, the type of work that occupied the enslaved, the nature of their master and mistress, and the amount of social freedoms and off-time bestowed upon them by the slave-holder. Many of the enslaved in North Carolina worked and lived together in small communities, making their immediate social world quite limited. When they sought to extend their social relationships, they were often required to look beyond their immediate surroundings and the confines of the plantation. Their social world often moved between and across plantations, and recollections from the formerly enslaved suggest that this was how enslaved men and women were able to manage their relationships and extend the limits of their social worlds and personal ties.

Several couples participated in crossplantation unions, where typically an enslaved woman and her children resided on a separate plantation to that of her partner and the father of her children. Isaac Johnson and his mother, Tilla, belonged to Jack Johnson, who owned a plantation in Lillington, on the north side of the Cape Fear River. Referring to his mother and father's relationship, Isaac remarked that his father, Bunch Matthews, did not belong to Jack Johnson and was in fact the slave of "old man Drew Matthews, a slave owner."[10] Isaac's narrative does not reveal whether Bunch lived near enough to him and Tilla to be able to visit them, yet several of the narratives do indicate that this type of arrangement was common.

Tempie Herndon Durham was enslaved in Chatham County and belonged to George Herndon. She described George Herndon's holdings as a "big plantation [where they] raised cawn, wheat, cotton an 'bacca. I don't know how many field niggers Marse George had, but he had a mess of dem."[11] Despite the "mess" of slaves George Herndon owned, Tempie was still compelled to look off the plantation when she sought to establish a family; she married Exter Durham, an enslaved man who resided on a neighboring plantation. She explained that on the night of their wedding Exter was unable to stay with her because "he belonged to Marse Snipes Durham an' he had to go back home." However, in an arrangement that seems to have been typical of many courtships and subsequent long-term relationships, Tempie explained that Exter would come and visit her during his free time on the weekends. "[H]e come back every Saturday night an' stay 'twell Sunday night."[12]

Slaves employed in the fields of the plantation may have been able to acquire a greater degree of independence and influence over their rights to off-time when compared to domestic slaves, who were employed in the houses of slaveholders. Certainly slaveholders attached a high value to their slaves who were employed within the domestic quarters or those who possessed a particular skill or trade. For example, according to the Davidson Family papers, a list of the slaves owned on the plantation in Iredell County revealed a slave named Henry, who was listed as a blacksmith and was priced at $1,200. Henry was counted as one of the most economically valuable slaves on the plantation, with the average value of other male slaves on the plantation ranging from $450 to $900.[13]

If a plantation was especially large the slaveholder required numerous slaves to work as domestics in the house or to be equipped with certain skills. Michael Cronly, who was based in Wilmington, listed several such slaves in his accounts written during 1865, including a cook, seamstress, nurse, chambermaid, baker, waitress, gardener, wood cutter, carriage driver, and carpenter.[14] Similarly, among the slaves on the McRae plantation in Fayetteville, there was a bricklayer, cook, coachman, blacksmith, and midwife listed in 1855.[15]

Despite the economic value placed on these members of the slave population by slaveholders, numerous sources reveal that the life of a enslaved domestic was often characterized by cruel and brutal treatment at the hands of the master and mistress. For example, Cornelia Andrews remembered being whipped in public for "breaking dishes an' being slow."[16] Severe and watchful mistresses could make the lives of house slaves particularly difficult. Ida Adkins, who was enslaved in Louisburg, Franklin County, recalled that her mistress, Mis' Mary Jane, was "quick as er whip-po'-will. She had black eyes dat snapped an' dey seed everythin'. She could turn her head so quick dat she'd ketch you every time you tried to steal a lump of sugar."[17] Enslaved domestics were also subject to the capricious whims of their masters and mistresses, as was the case in the household of Dr. Flint, the master of Harriet Jacobs. Jacobs recalled in her narrative that the cook of the household "never sent a dinner to his table without fear and trembling; for if there happened to be a dish not to his liking, he would either order her to be whipped, or compel her to eat every mouthful of it in his presence. The poor, hungry creature might not have objected to eating it; but she did object to having her master cram it down her throat till she choked."[18] Under the constant scrutiny of their master and mistress and required to be constantly available, day and night, to attend to their needs, enslaved domestics may have found their ability to manage their own personal lives severely curtailed.

Alongside the seemingly complete ownership of their time by the slaveholder, slaves were also subject to restrictions on their mobility. Working around the slave system, they made the best out of an impossible situation, managing their off-time as well as they could so that they could be in each other's company. Their lives, however, were subject to a set of formal and informal rules and regulations, which made this task all the more difficult. Measures such as slave codes, patrol gangs, and plantation justice were intended to control and contain the enslaved in the defined spaces of the plantation. Stephanie Camp argues that at the heart of the process of enslavement was a geographical impulse to locate the enslaved in plantation space.[19] The slave codes of North Carolina, first enacted in 1715 and then reinforced after 1741, were maintained and informally reinforced throughout the antebellum period. They sought to limit the movements of the slave beyond the physical boundaries of the plantation. These codes increasingly reflected southern white fears of an organized slave rebellion, and these fears were revealed in the restrictions imposed upon the slave's mobility and movement. Specific punishments were given to "any Negro or Negroes [who] shall presume to travel in the Night, or be found in the Quarters or Kitchens among other Persons' Negroes."[20] Any slave who was found to be off the plantation was expected to have a pass from his or her owner that detailed the name of the master or mistress and the origin and destination of their trip. They were required to produce the pass at the request of any white person.[21]

The slave codes also outlawed the meeting and socializing of slaves, again because of white fears concerning planned insurrections. This concern over the meeting of slaves was especially high in the urban centers of towns such as Wilmington, where a high proportion of the population was enslaved. In 1765, a Wilmington edict instructed that if any more than three slaves were seen together "on the streets, alleys, Vacant lots, House or other parts within this Borrough, playing, Riotting or Caballing on . . . Sunday, or any other day, or in the night time of any Day, whereby the Inhabitants or any of them may be disturbed or molested, the slave or slaves were to be apprehended, taken to the mayor, recorder, or any alderman and then committed or whipped, or both. The same act also imposed a ten o' clock curfew." Slaves had to acquire a pass from their master if they wished to be out beyond this hour.[22] These mechanisms of control were reinforced through the establishment of patrol gangs who rode through the local areas searching for and punishing any slaves found to be off the plantation without the required pass.[23]

The visiting rights of slaves, as laid down by the slaveholder could have a determining influence upon the personal relationships of the enslaved. Although some slaveholders were willing to make allowances in cases where their slaves were particularly isolated, this indulgence was usually underlined with an implicit assumption that "give the negro an inch, and he will surely take an ell."[24] Thus, as one planter recommends, "[o]n small farms where there are very few negroes, it may be proper to allow them to visit to a limited extent but in large plantations there can be no want of society, and consequently no excuse for visiting except among themselves." This writer further warns that enslaved men who were allowed to "run about all over neighborhood would rarely ever taken wives on the home plantation, merely wishing an excuse for their absence."[25]

These restrictions over the mobility of the enslaved were further reinforced through the physical boundaries erected on the plantation, which can be seen to represent the imposed geographical limits of enslaved life. Ironically, the work routines of the enslaved often involved the creation and maintenance of this defined and limited space. Louisa Adams recalled that on Tom Covington's plantation, where she was enslaved in Richmond County, "[a]ll de plantation was fenced in, dat is all de fields wid rails; de rails wuz ten feet long."[26] Similarly, Parker Pool, formerly enslaved in Wake County, recalled that "[d]ere wuz about

2000 acres in de plantation. All de farm lan' wuz fenced in wid wood rails."[27] The enslaved were then incorporated into creating and maintaining the "controlled and controlling landscapes that would determine the uses to which enslaved people put their bodies."[28]

The slaveholders contained the enslaved in defined and limited spaces, and thus opportunities for the enslaved to extend their social networks beyond that of the plantation increasingly narrowed. However, they were able to manage their personal lives by negotiating the existing systems of regulation and control. Certain social events that were organized and governed by the slaveholder and occurred as part of the work regimes on the plantation provided a context for the enslaved to "get out an play" and occasionally to "court all dey pleased."

A primary example of these opportunities is illustrated in the annual corn shucking held on numerous plantations, and to which slaveholders often invited a large number of the neighboring slaves. This invitation was a reciprocal agreement between the masters of the respective slaves. By inviting a large number of slaves from local plantations to join in the shucking the slaveholder ensured that the maximum quantity of corn could be husked in the least amount of time. These events were a significant element in the social world of the enslaved, heralding various opportunities for them to catch the eye of a prospective suitor within an authorized social space on the plantation.

Formerly enslaved men and women recalled events such as corn shuckings with the emphasis on their social element rather than the work involved. Henry Rountree described such events as the "grandes time ever. We has two er three corn shuckings ever fall, we has wood splittin' days an' invite de neighbors in de winter time. De wimmen has quiltin's an' dat night we has a dance."[29] Indeed, one significant aspect of these shuckings was courtship, and several enslaved men and women recalled courtship games as a prominent part of the night's proceedings. Julius Nelson remembered the shuckings at his master's plantation in Anson County, where "de person what fin's a red year (ear of corn) can kiss who dey pleases."[30] Tanner Spikes also recalled kissing for a red ear of corn. "I 'members a corn shuckin' what happened 'fore de war wus over, an' what a time dem niggers did have. Dey kisses when dey fin' a red year an' atter dat dey pops some popcorn an dey dances ter de music od de banjo."[31]

Occasions such as these not only allowed for the enslaved to flirt with each other, size each other up and down, and determine who they had taken a fancy to, but as Anna Wright, in the opening vignette of this chapter suggested, they also provided the opportunity for couples who were already in a relationship to "get out and play and court all they pleased." Of course, these approved social events had alternative functions for the slaveholder themselves. They emphasized their paternalistic image to the local white community and fellow slaveholders and also served to regulate the leisure time of the slaves. Slaveholders were aware of the significance of such occasions to their slave community, and it is no coincidence that these events were often arranged after a period of heavy or intense labor. Yet, simply because these licensed social events were governed and authorized by the slaveholder does not mean that the enslaved did not derive any personal or emotional fulfillment from them.

James Walvin argues that slaveholders encouraged the process of rational recreation among their slaves as a means to integrate them further into the systems of labor operating on the plantations of the South. Rational recreation is defined as periods of leisure time where slaves were engaged in endeavors that were useful yet pleasurable.[32] At social events such as corn shuckings and candy pullings, the enslaved can be seen to have engaged in a form of rational recreation which met the labor demands of the plantation yet contained an element of recreational activity. Furthermore, Walvin also suggests that "slaves like workers elsewhere, might subvert the system and convert it to their ends and impose on it a style which was all their own."[33]

The enslaved certainly did subvert and convert the system to their own ends. Within the collective memories of enslavement these events were recalled with the emphasis on the respite from daily toil and the enjoyment the participants experienced. Henry James Trentham discussed these events with a degree of enthusiasm and excitement. "De corn shuckin's wus a great time. Marster gave good licker to everybody den. . . . We had big suppers den an' a good time at corn shuckin's."[34] One significant element of events such as corn shuckings was the presence of the fiddler. Many mentioned him as one of the central figures at these social gatherings. Bill Crump, who was enslaved in Davidson County, remarked with a mixture of pride and excitement on his father's role at the local frolics: "My daddy was a fiddler, an' he sometimes played for de dances at de Cross Roads, a little village near de marster's place . . . yes ma'm, we had our fun at de dances, co'n chuckins, candy pullin's, an de gatherin's an' we sarbed de marster better by habin' our fun."[35]

The slaveholder's purpose in allowing their slaves to attend these social gatherings, listen to the fiddler, socialize, and dance was not lost on enslaved men such as Bill. He understood that these occasions were controlled and regulated by the slaveholder, and in allowing their slaves to attend these events the slaveholder would expect a more obedient and pliable workforce. The ownership of a expert fiddler was heartily recommended by one planter writing in the pages of *De Bow's Review*, "I have a good fiddler, and keep him well supplied with catgut, and I make it his duty to play for the negroes every Saturday night until 12 o'clock. . . . Charley's fiddle is always accompanied with Ihurod on the triangle and Sam to 'pat'."[36] The enjoyment that the enslaved derived from these dances is evident, despite slaveholder and slave both being aware of the ulterior motives underpinning the event. "Sat'day nigh dance at de plantation wuz jist de finest ting we wanted in dem days."[37] The distinction between work-based and nonwork-based events is reflected in the comments of those who felt deprived of periods of off-time. Clara Jones recalled that on Mr. Felton McGee's place in Wake County where she had been enslaved, *"we ain't had no fun dar,* case hit takes all of our strength ter do our daily task."[38] Cornelia Andrews, also used a similar frame of reference to describe her days on Doctor McKay Vaden's plantation, *"We ain't had much fun,* nothin' but candy pullin's 'bout onct a year."[39]

These periods of licensed leisure formed part of an informal social contract governing the relationship between the enslaved and the slaveholder. They were perceived as a necessary release from the perspective of the slaveholder, who envisaged a well behaved and obedient workforce through the promise of future such occasions. Yet, while these occasions functioned as part of the slave system and in many ways helped to maintain it, the enslaved came to expect such obligations from their master and mistress and embraced such opportunities when the chance arose. Not every slaveholder was willing to concede such time to their slave population, and it was telling that for the slaves who were not provided with such opportunities they characterized their life as comparably worse than those enslaved men and women who were provided with authorized occasions of recreation.

Events such as corn shuckings represented part of a distinct calendar of social events that were governed by the slaveholder, reflecting the respective peaks and troughs in the agricultural year. Although a certain amount of these events tended to occur within the confines of the plantation, usually under the auspices of the slaveholder or the overseer, others were staged away from the home plantation. During holiday periods such as Christmas, or at layby time, which usually coincided with the white community's celebration of Independence Day, the enslaved were often given off-time and permission to leave the plantation. By July 4, the corn was laid by and the wheat stored, and many of the formerly enslaved recalled this period as a holiday, marking the end of the planting season. Henry James Trentham, who was enslaved near Camden and belonged to Dr. Trentham, remembered this period known as "lay-by," which occurred around the Fourth of July. He recalled that, "at lay-by time was another big time. Dat wus 'bout de fourth of July. Dey give a big dinner an' everbody et all de barbecue an' cake dey wanted."[40] Ransom Sidney Taylor also recollected that on John Cane's plantation in Wake County, the slaves had holidays "at layby time and the 4th of July."[41] John Cane reportedly owned sixty slaves but Ransom Taylor further recalled that "marster only kept seven on the plantation with him."[42] Thus, these holiday periods would have provided an opportunity for Cane's slaves to perhaps reacquaint themselves with friends, lovers, or family members also owned by him but who didn't reside on the home plantation.

Similarly, Christmas was a particularly significant period for the enslaved as they acquired relaxed social freedoms, and perhaps more significant, increased mobility. Alice Baugh's mother, Ferbie, who had been enslaved in Edgecombe County, reportedly told her that during the Christmas holidays, which lasted from Saturday to Monday, the enslaved were allowed to go "up de riber to other plantations ter dances an' all dem things."[43] During the Christmas holidays when the social order was temporarily eased, the mobility and leisure time of the enslaved increased, and their social freedoms extended it afforded the enslaved the opportunity to attend social events at which would be numerous other enslaved men and women from the local area. Such freedoms and the relaxation of the regulations governing their daily lives were illustrated by the enslaved at the John Kooner parades, performed annually during the Christmas period. These parades were a festive undertaking but appear to have had little religious or spiritual component to them. They instead consisted of groups of the enslaved (typically men rather than women) inverting the social order by dressing up in traditional West African costumes, parading around the plantation, and requesting money from their master and mistress. This was commonly undertaken by African and African Caribbean slaves in several parts of the West Indies, particularly in Jamaica, where the custom of parading continues until the present day.[44] However, on the North American mainland the only place where the tradition of John Kooner is known to have persisted among the enslaved was North Carolina. Given the composition of the slave population in this state and the fact that a majority of slaves imported into North Carolina came overland from Virginia and South Carolina, it is perhaps surprising that there are no known references to the John Kooner parade in the neighboring towns of Charleston or Richmond. However, the majority of those slaves that were imported directly into North Carolina were from the West Indies, especially from the island of Jamaica, and this may help in part to resolve this matter.[45]

The most detailed account of the parade was given by Doctor Edward Warren, who witnessed a John Kooner while visiting Josiah Collin's Somerset Plantation, which lay on the shores of Lake Scuppernong in Washington County. His description of the John Kooners was made during a visit to Somerset in 1829. He observed that the Kooners only appeared during Christian festivals, most notably on Christmas day. The leading figure was the ragman, who was dressed in a costume of rags, adorned by two great ox horns, attached to the skin of a raccoon, which was drawn over his head and face. The ragman was also decorated with bells and strings of goat horns "so arranged as to jingle at every movement; and a short stick of seasoned wood, carried in his hands." Followed by the ragman came the second leading character of the parade, who, according to Dr. Warren was, "the best looking darkey of the place, who wears no disguise, but is simply arrayed in what they call his Sunday-go-to-meeting suit and carries in his hand a small bowl or tin cup, while the other parts are appropriated by some half a dozen fellows, each arrayed fantastically in ribbons, rags, and feathers, and bearing between them several so-called musical instruments or 'gumba boxes,' which consist of wooden frames covered over with tanned sheep skins."[46] The parade took the form of a dance, accompanied by a song directed at the master.

At the end of the verse the second character approached the master with his bowl in hand to receive the expected quarter. The procession then moved on to finally come to rest in the slave quarters.

The John Kooner parades excited much amusement and wonder among the slaveholders and their families. Anne Cameron wrote to her husband Paul from Fairintosh Plantation, Orange County, on January 8, 1848. She delighted in telling him of the Christmas they had enjoyed and remarked how "[o]ur little ones keep well and are as happy as the day is long. . . . They all had a merry Christmas finding their stockings full of St Nicholas' gifts upon waking and having music and dancing together with a John O'Cooner."[47] In later years, Rebecca Cameron recalled the Christmases she had spent at her grandfather's rice plantation on the Cape Fear River. She wrote that "[o]n the second day after Christmas the John Coonahs began to make their appearance. Sometime in the course of the morning, an ebony herald, breathless with excitement, would project the announcement: De John Coonahs comin! And away flew every pair of feet within nursery precincts."[48]

Evidently the procession lacked any real significance to the amused white children and adults who failed to understand the deeper meanings behind the parade. Elizabeth Fenn argues that the John Kooners functioned on Christmas day to invert the traditional roles and positions that white and black occupied in the normal social hierarchy of the South. She considers the celebrations in terms of a "cathartic, steam-valve function" helping to ease the social tensions that existed between the white and black populations of the slave-holding states.[49] The description of the Kooner parades provided by Harriet Jacobs certainly seems to support Fenn's argument. She wrote, "They consist of companies of slaves from the plantations, generally of the lower class. . . . For a month previous they are composing songs, which are sung on this occasion. These companies, of a hundred each, turn out early in the morning, and are allowed to go round till twelve o'clock, begging for contributions. Not a door is left unvisited where there is the least chance of obtaining a penny or a glass of rum. They do not drink while they are out, but carry the rum home in jugs, to have a carousal."[50]

The very fact that the men who participated in the parade observed by Jacobs were described as "*of the lower class*" suggests that they sought a complete reversal of the southern hierarchy in the Kooner parades, not only in their relationships with white southerners but also within their relationships with each other. In addition, the John Kooners were reported as *carry*[ing] *the rum home in jugs, to have a carousal*, emphasizing the extent to which they cultivated a sense of extended kinship and community life, sharing their spoils with the wider enslaved community on the plantation. Fenn also suggests that although slaveholders encouraged these events in the hope that they would contribute to the fostering of a more placid and docile slave population, the enslaved community manipulated such occasions, expressing their hopes and fears through ridicule and costume. She writes, "[C]ostumes . . . were mere emblems of the more profound role reversal that Jonkonnu could entail. Blacks saw in the festivities a chance not only to 'dress' in white skin but also to claim white social prerogatives."[51] These white social prerogatives would have included the right to control their own destiny, determining the uses to which they put their bodies, both in laboring for themselves and in determining who had the right to share in that labor, also enjoying their own bodies, sharing them with somebody within public and private spaces, not as a site of profit and sadistic abuse, but as a place which these men and women would have called home—in the nape of their lover's neck, in the gentle kiss planted firmly on their lips, in the comfort of their arms. Nevertheless, the enslaved were still subject to plantation regulation and the governance of the master and mistress during these periods. Leaving the plantation still required a pass issued by the slaveholder which specified the slave's destination and the expiry date. Even when the slaveholder permitted the enslaved to visit other plantations, the extent of their social freedoms was still limited by the pass system, signifying the fact that the enslaved were part of plantation property, even if temporarily removed from its physical confines.

In addition, the ways in which the enslaved spent their holiday period was subject to the precarious whims of the slaveholder, who could refuse permission for the enslaved to even leave the plantation. Henry Burgwyn, writing from Boston to his overseer on his plantation in Northampton County, granted his slaves two days holiday as a reward after they had laid by the crop, but he instructed his overseer that "they must not go off the plantation they must work their own crops."[52] Similarly, Charles Pettigrew restricted the movement of his slave population during the Christmas holidays on his two plantations, Belgrade and Magnolia in Washington County. Because of trouble between his own and some neighboring slaves, he instructed his two overseers that "[I think] the people had better stay at home during Christmas holydays; no good can result from their going to the lake & it might be that some evil would. . . . My idea is stay at home & mind your business & let other people mind theirs."[53]

Pettigrew's actions underlined how instrumental the slaveholder was in shaping the ways in which the enslaved were able to manage their intimate relationships. The enslaved populations on Pettigrew's plantations were by no means small. For example, in 1859 he listed 56 slaves living at Magnolia.[54] However, Pettigrew was evidently aware that his punishment would have been sorely felt within the quarters of the enslaved. His actions served to deny the enslaved their expected social privileges during the festive season, including those of socializing, possible courtships, and the pleasures of human interaction, while at the same time enhancing his own image as an authoritarian and masterful slaveholder. When these privileges were not forthcoming during the holiday period the mobility of the enslaved was severely restricted and consequently limited to the spaces of the plantation.

It was often within the confines of these defined spaces then that the en-slaved were able to create a semiautonomous social world; one that was autho-rized and overseen by the slaveholder. However, the enslaved also developed distinct and separate social spheres that transcended the spatial and temporal limits that regulated their lives. They were sometimes able to court in spaces that were hidden from the slaveholder's direct gaze, in locations that renegoti-ated the physical confines that regulated their lives. They often stole away from plantation space to ensure that they could pursue their romantic relationships on their own terms.

Stealing away from the plantation at night to attend a secret frolic or to en-gage in a particular courtship represented a means by the enslaved to establish alternative geographies of courtship. Stephanie Camp argues that these "rival geographies" were characterized by motion and represented the "secret move-ment of bodies, objects and information within and around plantation space."[55] The enslaved sought to create a social world on their own terms, removed from the defined places and spaces of the plantation. They provided meaning to these places and spaces, what one recent scholar terms "enslaved landscapes," by using them and investing them with life. These landscapes "became the backdrop of human action" as the enslaved struggled to shape their lives on their own terms.[56] While they were willing to appropriate the time given by the slaveholder dur-ing authorized events, they also sought to define visual and cultural worlds that were distinct and separate from that of the plantation and the authority of the slaveholder.[57]

These illegitimate social gatherings were not always physically removed from the plantation itself. They could, for example, have occurred in the quarters of the enslaved. Ann Parker, who was enslaved in Wake County to Abner Parker, revealed that during slavery she used to visit "neighborin' plantations whar we'd sing an' talk an' maybe dance."[58] Holding social gatherings and parties in areas designated as their living space, the enslaved attempted to create some psycho-logical distance between their world and that of their masters and mistresses. They were actively reclaiming these spaces as their own, places where they could truly experience themselves as human beings.[59]

Other social gatherings were organized away from the confines of the plan-tation, and several enslaved men and women recollected that despite being unable to obtain permission from the slaveholder to attend, coupled with the threats posed by the local patrol gangs, they would still find a way to be present. Leon Berry recalled that his father, Hugh, who was enslaved in Long Creek, would frequently leave the plantation, negotiating the local terrain to attend these par-ties. The primary reason motivating young men and women to leave the planta-tion after dark and expose themselves to the threat of the patrol gangs was the possibilities of establishing romantic relationships. As Hugh Berry recounted, "I'm goin' back over there to see that girl. And then they said and you gonna go too, said they goin' over there to see the girls and the first thing they know say, here come the patterollers!"[60]

Threats much bigger than that of the patrol gangs could sometimes be posed, however, occasionally with tragic consequences. Following a move to Georgia from Greene County, North Carolina, Guildford, a slave belonging to the turpentine planter Ben Williams, died following his bid to attend a local frolic after a day's work. Ben's wife Sarah wrote to her parents explaining the tragedy. "[Y]ou know it is against the law for them to go without a pass from their master or overseer nevertheless they do go, & some of our turpentine hands will work all day and then walk eight or ten miles to dance all night. Well Guilford undertook to go got lost in the woods and wandered for nearly six days . . . he lingered about a week and then died. We did not know that he was missing until he had been out three days."[61] Not knowing the surrounding landscape of the new plantation in Georgia, Guildford understandably lost his way. However, separated from all that he knew and loved on the home plantation in North Carolina, he was evidently determined to craft new places and spaces, his own landscape, upon which he could provide meaning to his life as a member of the enslaved community in his new home. Sarah Hicks Williams's comment that "we did not know that he was missing until he had been out three days" underlines the complete disregard with which some slaveholder's thought about their human chattel; it also, however, suggests the ease with which the enslaved might have slipped away without the slaveholder noticing their absence. As long as they were back by morning and fit for work, the slaveholder might have been none the wiser.

How their slaves spent their evenings certainly troubled men and women of the slaveholding classes. One planter wrote in an article for the *Southern Cultivator* that "[o]ne of the most important regulations on a farm is to see that the hands get plenty of sleep." He regarded his labor force as "thoughtless, and if allowed to do so, will stay up late at night." To remedy this tendency, the writer suggested that a large cowbell be used to serve as a signal for bedtime among the slaves, which he stipulated should fall at least by ten o'clock."[62] Slaveholder James Hinton also tried this practice of tying cowbells around the necks of slave men to prevent them leaving the plantation at night to court. This was to no avail as Penny Williams, formerly enslaved to Hinton herself, explained, "Dar wus some nigger mens what 'ud go courtin' spite of de debil." Reveling in their "ingenuity," she recalled that "Dey ain't got sense nuff ter put dere han's in de bell ter keep de clapper from ringin', but dey does stuff de bell wid leaves an' it doan ring none, 'sides dat dey tears deir shirts, or steals sheets from missus clothes line an' fold dem ter make a scarf. Dey ties dese roun' deir necks ter hide de bell an' goes on a-courtin'."[63]

The central issues concerning their slaves' courtship practices were tied to slaveholders' larger concerns of property rights and ownership. These issues were landscapes upon which the slaveholder and the enslaved competed for and con-tested claims of power and authority over the ownership of the enslaved per-son's body and time. Straddling these authorized and illicit geographies were the social and temporal spaces which religious worship afforded the enslaved. His-torians have already provided strong evidence that by the 1830s African Ameri-cans were playing a major part in shaping the religious cultures of the new world.[64] Regardless of legislation and church regulations to the contrary, Prot-estant churches continued to allow blacks to preach after 1830 and the insur-rections of the previous decade, albeit under the watchful eyes of their white brethren. Black preaching continued in biracial churches, and the enslaved pur-sued their religious activities within these institutions as well as at camp meet-ings and other biracial religious events.[65]

The authority of African American preachers was never completely destroyed in the quarters of the enslaved either, and enslaved Christians created their own invisible and semiautonomous churches, as described by Albert Raboteau in his classic analysis of the *Invisible Institution* within enslaved life.[66] Using both the authorized and illicit social spaces of religious worship, they were able to make use of the Protestant faith as a physical and psychological social space. As well as the obvious spiritual strength it no doubt provided them, it also enabled them to extend their social relationships, interacting and socializing with other enslaved men and women on a more informal level. Slaveholder Kemp Plummer Battle, who had owned plantations in Edgecombe County, recognized this feature of slave life when he pointed out the problem that his neighbor had when he ap-pointed a chaplain on his plantation, intended for his slaves' spiritual growth. He commented that "they found it irksome in comparison with frequenting the neighboring churches of their choice where they could meet their friends from other plantations"[67]

The fact that black people, both enslaved and free, were separated off from the white congregation in church, by rails, or by seating them in separate areas, would have likely helped to facilitate this particular aspect of church attendance for this section of the congregation. For example, at their monthly meeting in October 1816, the Sawyers Creek Baptist Church agreed that a "door be made on the west side of the House for the Black people."[68] Making the enslaved and free persons of color enter the church through a separate doorway was no doubt intended to enforce racial segregation in the church and remind them that al-though God perceived all humanity as equal, the majority of white southern churchgoers certainly did not. The enslaved who entered through a doorway separate from the one their master and mistress used may have found a few stolen moments to pass pleasantries, catch the eye of an admirer, or introduce themselves to members of the enslaved community with whom they were un-acquainted.

A number of formerly enslaved men and women also recollected that at the church of their master and mistress they were seated separately from the white congregation. Reverend Squire Dowd, who had been enslaved in Moore County, remarked that "[o]n Sundays we went to the white folk's church. We sat in a barred off place, in the back of the church or the gallery."[69] Others among the enslaved also remembered being seated at the back of the church or in a corner or a specific space to themselves.[70] Although few details emerge here regarding the forms and extent of communication between the enslaved within the social space of the church, it is difficult not to imagine them employing such opportunities to their own advantages. Although they were not completely away from the observance of the master and mistress, they were, by virtue of being seated at the back, out of their sight. Away from the direct gaze of the slaveholders the enslaved would have taken this opportunity to silently communicate with other enslaved men and women—perhaps through facial expressions, stolen glances, and whispered words.[71]

Enslaved men and women could also use the places of the church to see their courtships progress. Barbara Haywood, who had been enslaved in Wake County, recalled that after meeting her future spouse, Frank, as a young girl at one of her master's corn shuckings, that she "seed Frank a few times at de Holland's Methodist Church whar we went to church wid our white folks."[72] The church served as one of the social and temporal spaces in which Barbara and Frank's courtship could have progressed, where they could have seen each other and shared stolen moments, albeit in an authorized and very public social space.

Similarly, Lucy Ann Dunn, whose relationship with Jim was cited in the previous chapter, recalled that "It wus in de little Baptist Church at Neuse whar I first seed big black Jim Dunn an' I fell in love wid him den, I reckons." The Baptist church provided Lucy Ann and Jim with the opportunity to continue courting over quite a lengthy period of time, meeting every Sunday at church. Their courtship eventually culminated in a marriage ceremony a year later.[73] Although Lucy Ann and Jim's relationship occurred in the immediate aftermath of emancipation, the way in which they conducted their relationship, using the church as their courting ground, and the matter-of-fact way in which Lucy Ann referred to this element of their relationship suggests that this was an accepted and frequent feature of life before, as well as after, emancipation.

The social worlds of the enslaved were then constructed within various social and temporal spaces. These spaces and places overlapped and intertwined, imbued with alternative and competing meanings. As the enslaved navigated the choppy and often terrifying waters of courtship they were also required to negotiate their ways around the more formal measures structuring their lives. Although they did manage to facilitate and maintain their romantic relationships from within the slave system, they also established an alternative geography of courtship where they could experience themselves as people, individuals, and human beings. These social and temporal spheres resisted the slaveholder's control over their intimate lives. It also served to redefine the concepts of space and time that the system of slavery imposed upon them. The transgression of the spatial and temporal boundaries of the plantation represented a bid by the enslaved to establish meaningful relationships that were detached from the daily realities of enslaved life. The autonomous social spaces defined and shaped by them were simultaneous with the authorized free time provided by the slaveholder, and they were thus able to broaden the margins of their own lives in both these spheres. Yet the creation of distinct and separate social spaces by the enslaved, within which they were able to enjoy each other in various and multiple ways, represented their desire to reclaim this intimate aspect of their lives and consequently resist the slaveholder's assumed rights to regulate and control their emotional lives.

4

Taking a Whipping for Lily
Courtship as a Narrative of Resistance

LILY PERRY was an assertive and defiant woman enslaved on a plantation belonging to Jerry Perry in Franklin County. Recalling her bold retaliations to the punishments received at the hands of her master and the overseer, she remarked, "When dey'd start ter whup me I'd bite lak a run-mad dog so dey'd chain my han's. See hyar, hyars de scars made by de chains. Dey'd also pick me up by de years, an flin' me foun' (around)." Lily's future spouse, Robert, must have felt every lash of the whip; he pleaded with Lily to behave in the way that the slaveholder demanded of her. She explained, "I know how he uster hate ter see me git dem beatin's an' he'd beg me not ter let my mouth be so sassy, but I can't help hit." Driven by his feelings for Lily, Robert used to take her beatings whenever he could "an' a heap of times he sneak out ter de fiel's in de ebenin an' toted dat slops ter de pigs."

Referring to a specific incident when Robert attempted to take a whipping for her, she recalled that "Onct when marster wus whuppin me Robert run up an' begged marse ter put de whuppin' on him 'stead of me. De result wus marse whupped us both an' we 'cided ter run away. We did run away but night brought us back ter another whuppin' an' we ain't neber run away no mo'."[1] Lily and Robert's courtship serves as a poignant illustration of the competing and conflicting power relations that lay at the heart of enslaved courtships. As the previous chapter underlined, enslaved courtships were orchestrated on shifting terrains, largely occurring within the rigidly defined boundaries of a slave system, which was established, maintained, and protected by white southern society. The slave body was generally contained and detained within the spaces controlled by the slaveholder. Although periods of licensed leisure provided the enslaved with the opportunity to indulge in a limited sense of enjoyment, these events were organized on the slaveholder's terms, and consequently during these periods they remained subject to the regulations of the master and mistress.

To actively pursue and conduct a courting relationship on their own terms, enslaved men and women had to resist and renegotiate the power relationships that structured this system. They were thus engaged in a constant struggle with the slaveholder to define the shape and nature of their courting experiences.

Consequently, courtship should be read as part of a wider discourse of resistance for the enslaved, as they sought to subvert and undermine the systems of authority that shaped their emotional lives and to replace it with a style that was all their own. Resistance, as Stephanie Camp argues, should not be understood in terms of a division between "material and political issues on the one hand and aesthetic, spiritual and intimate (emotionally and physically) issues on the other." Rather, the politics of the enslaved were shaped by daily and often covert acts of resistance that contested and challenged the networks of power and domination within which the southern slave system implicated them. This particular understanding of resistance is particularly relevant for the enslaved in the American South where, James Scott maintains, "These practices, which rarely if ever called into question the system of slavery *as such*, nevertheless achieved far more in their unannounced, limited and truculent way than the few heroic and brief armed uprisings about which so much has been written."[2] Certain actions of the enslaved within the arena of courtship can be understood in terms of these daily and often covert acts of resistance. The acts usually had no wider impact than on the immediate social world of the enslaved, yet they represented an implicit rejection of the rules of regulation and control that structured the experiences of enslavement in the South, most particularly in relation to the slaveholder's assumed rights over the emotional dynamics of enslaved life.

As one scholar of slavery recently argues, enslaved men faced grave risks and problems in making unauthorized visits to their families on separate plantations and the threat of punishment posed by the patrol gangs and the slaveholder "suggests the position of [enslaved] husbands and fathers as protectors and risk-takers."[3] For several reasons enslaved women found their mobility rather more contained than that of their male counterparts. Often they had responsibilities to children or families, which tied them to the plantation and prevented them from leaving to visit their lovers and their families. Work regimes on the plantation also detained enslaved women, who were typically located in the fields or the plantation house.[4] Even enslaved women who had acquired skills as seamstresses or midwifes did not usually have to leave the plantation for their labor to be exploited by the slaveholder.[5]

The nature of skilled occupations for some enslaved men meant they were able to hire themselves out, receiving wages and paying their master or mistress an amount each month for the privilege of owning their own time. Through this practice they were able to obtain a higher degree of mobility than enslaved women, whose occupations typically grounded them within the borders of the plantation. Hannah Plummer's father was a stonecutter in Wake County. Although she and her mother belonged to a different owner, Hannah's father still lived with his wife and child courtesy of his occupation. Hannah explained that "he hired his time and gave it to his missus and lived with us."[6] Anderson Henderson's master, John Henderson, allowed him to hire out his labor. Anderson was given the choice to be hired by the month or the year and so he explained to his master, "I thought as it is more customary in Wilmington to be hire[d] by the month than the year that I would go by the month at 12 dollars per month." Anderson's awareness of the freedom that the terms of hiring bestowed upon him were further revealed when he wrote that he had decided to be paid monthly rather than yearly because "if I did not like one house I could go to another for this is a good many hotels here that I could get in if I did not like this."[7]

Another element of life that tied enslaved women to the plantation was childbirth and parenting. Deborah Gray White illustrates that the majority of slave runaways were between sixteen and thirty-five years old. She points out that during this period most enslaved women were either pregnant, nursing a child, or had a small child to care for. Thus, as White explains, slave women were less mobile than men and ran away from the plantation less frequently because "women tended to be more concerned with the welfare of their children, and this limited their mobility. Fugitive men loved their offspring, but unlike the runaway male, the slave woman who left her children behind could not be certain that they would be given the best possible care."[8]

Despite the geographical mobility of enslaved men, they were still required to devise methods to evade and outwit the local patrollers if they wanted to see their lovers more than just the customary once a week. The patrol gangs did not ride out every night, however, and it was this element of not knowing when or where the patrollers would turn up that presented such a threat to the enslaved. In Rowan County, for example, regulations of 1825 stated, "It shall be their duty, or two of their number, at least to patrol their respective districts once in every week; in failure thereof, they shall be subject to the penalties prescribed by law."[9] However, unannounced night rides during the week ensured that the threat of the patroller was always present in the minds of the enslaved population. In evading the patrol gangs, enslaved men demonstrated their resistance to the measures that restricted their movements and consequently manipulated their emotional lives. Hugh Berry and his companions, discussed in the previous chapter, were fully aware of the threat that the patrol gang posed to their personal safety, yet they persisted in leaving the plantation after dark in order to "*see the girls.*"

They faced severe dangers in confronting the patrollers, who were aware of their authority over the slave and who lost no opportunity to exploit this in their favor. Blount Baker, who had been enslaved in Wilson County, recalled his experiences of the ways in which the patrol gangs manipulated the emotional needs and desires of the enslaved. He explained, "I know once a patteroller tol' me dat iffen I'd give him a belt I found *dat he'd let me go by ter see my gal dat night*, but when he kotch me dat night he whupped me."[10] The patrol gangs were fully conscious of their own authority, and they were not reluctant to abuse their positions at the expense of the physical safety and emotional well being of the enslaved.

Often the slaveholder resented the patrol gang's encroachment of their own authority over their slave population and consequently the power of the patrollers was mediated by the influence of the slaveholders. The enslaved were occasionally able to use the leverage of the slaveholder against the patrol gangs; hence, it is possible to see the contradictory and conflicting relations of power that structured enslaved life. In Blount Baker's case he informed his master of the situation, and the patroller was made to give the belt to Master Henry, who gave Blount a possum for it. Blount's actions represented an explicit means of retaliation against the patroller. By informing his master of the event, Blount was able to exploit his relationship with the slaveholder to his own advantage. Master Henry's handling of this situation, however, may have been the consequence of his own feelings that his authority had been undermined rather than an expression of his paternalism or benevolence. Although the actions of Master Henry underlined his ultimate authority over both Blount and the patroller, the case also illustrates the ways in which the enslaved might appropriate the power of the slaveholder for their own ends.

The threat from the patrol gangs was explicit, however, and these local white men exercised their authority with a zeal that perhaps exposed their limited access to power in the wider public domain. Harriet Jacobs remarked that the patrol provided a "grand opportunity for the low whites to scourge. They exulted in such a chance to exercise a little brief authority."[11] Patrol regulations sanctioned corporal punishment as in the Act of Assembly of 1794, which stated that "the patrollers in each district, or a majority of those present, shall have power to inflict a punishment not exceeding fifteen lashes, on all slaves they may find off their owner's plantation, or traveling on the Sabbath, or other unreasonable time, without a proper permit or pass."[12]

John Bectom recalled the harsh punishments that the patrol gangs would dish out to any slave found away from the plantation without a pass. Referring to the secret dances and parties his enslaved grandmother had attended, he remarked, "While they would be there the patterollers would visit them. Sometimes the patterollers whipped all they caught at this place, all they set their hands on, unless they had a pass."[13] W. L. Bost remembered how the patrol gangs gave out their punishments: "If you wasn't in your proper place when the paddyrollers come they lash you 'til' you was black and blue. The women got 15 lashes and the men 30. That is for jes bein' out without a pass."[14]

The enslaved typically reacted in an implicit and covert manner against the rules and regulations that ultimately detained them on the plantation. They evaded the patrol gangs and rejected the slaveholder's rules. Courtships continued under the cloak of secrecy and the cover of darkness. For example, Celia Robinson was born on the McKnight plantation, in Louisburg, Franklin County. Her father, however, lived on a neighboring plantation belonging to Dr. Wiley Perry. Celia recalled the story told to her by her parents of how her father was able to make unauthorized visits to her mother in spite of warnings from the patrollers by developing secret signs that indicated his arrival. "I 'member when my father would come ter see mother. De patterollers tole him if he didn't stop coming home so much dey was goin' to whip him. He had a certain knock on de door den mother would let him in."[15] The system of secret signs to indicate the arrival of one's lover reflects the subversive and alternative means of communication, the *hidden transcripts*, between enslaved couples, which served to strengthen understanding and intimacy between them.[16] The nature of their relationship demanded that Celia's mother and father develop their own secret codes, understood only by the young courting couple and essential for the continuance of their relationship. It is significant that the courting relationship was characterized not only by the secret movement of people but also by covert means of communicating with each other, thus underlining how these couples managed to carry on their romance in spite of the rules and regulations that structured their lives.

Other members of the formerly enslaved from across the South recalled the ways in which courting couples would develop means to evade the patrol gangs by incorporating the help of other members of the enslaved community. Henry Green from Arkansas explained how a group of enslaved women would help courting couples if the patrollers made an appearance on the home plantation and the young man was there without a pass. He explained how they would "raise er loose plank in de flo whut dey done made loose fer this berry puppus, en de nigggger he den drop right down quick down 'neath de flo twix de jists, en de wimmen den slap de plank right bak in place on top er de man ter hide him."[17] Courtship was very much a public affair within the quarters of the enslaved. Enslaved men and women had an interest in new relationships because they were the future of these communities; fragile and subject to forces that they had little control over, men and women within enslaved communities across the South sought to help courtships flourish when they could, supporting these couples through their practical help as well as their guiding advice.

In spite of the threat of the patrol gangs, the whippings promised by the overseer, and the preventative measures taken by the slaveholder to detain his slaves on the plantation, enslaved men carried on their courtships. In their longing to see their heart's desire, to tell their lovers, and show them, that there was one above all who would always put them first, these couples were required to negotiate their ways around the larger systems that shaped their lives.

Honor, courage, and boldness were celebrated aspects of masculinity for both enslaved and free in the antebellum South. These aspects of masculinity were undoubtedly rooted in enslaved men's West African heritage, where various and differing warrior rituals were integrated into the norms of various societies.[18] The pursuit of a courtship and all this involved for enslaved men, in terms of escaping and evading the patrol gangs, allowed them the opportunity to enhance their own sense of masculine identity and resist the negative gender characteristics that had been imposed upon them in the context of slavery. To court and hence display their masculine prowess, they were first required to overcome the physical obstacles presented by the patrol gangs. Sam T. Stewart recalled that, in slavery days, "we set traps to catch the patterollers. . . . [W]e stretched grape vines across the roads, then we would run from them. They would follow, and get knocked off their horses."[19] Lizzie Baker also recalled her father telling her of this practice. "I remember Pap tellin' me 'bout stretchin' vines across roads and paths to knock de paterollers off deir horses when dey were tryin' to ketch slaves."[20] These practices of evasion helped to cultivate a sense of camaraderie among enslaved men, who were united in their efforts to undermine and outsmart the patrollers to win their chance to pursue their romantic relationships. Hugh Berry, whose daring exploits were recounted in the previous chapter, stressed that a key aspect of his account was escaping the patrol gangs: "Every two or three nights, we'd go out, four or five of us, would get together and go out. We'd get out and the first thing you know is here comes the patterollers."[21] The contest of courtship and the essence of resistance that structured many courtship experiences served to bolster enslaved men's sense of masculine identity, not only in the context of an intimate union but also between enslaved men themselves.

Sometimes enslaved men would act alone rather than in groups against the patrol gangs. Individual tales of trickery and cunning became known throughout enslaved communities across the South, remembered and relived in their mind's eye as part of the collective histories of enslavement. These stories emphasize the masculine image of enslaved men who actively resisted or challenged the patrol gangs, positioning them in the role of "trickster," as they outwitted their rivals through the use of their quick thinking and resourcefulness as opposed to brute force and physical strength. The "trickster" character can be found in several of these recollections. According to one narrative derived from the formerly enslaved, Jim had been fooling his master for seven years, pretending that he was too sick to work. Because of his alleged ailments, Jim had been gaining better rations and increased respite from work. However, his behavior was a source of annoyance to other enslaved men on the plantation, and they decided to inform the master of his fakery. They insisted to the master that if he would visit Jim after breakfast he would see the deceit for himself. According to the tale, the master headed down to Jim's quarters, where he found Jim sitting in the chair, playing his fiddle, and singing the following tune: "Hello, fool ole marster seven years, I'm gonna fool 'im seven more." When the master opened the door and revealed himself to Jim, it was reported that "Jim fell over on the floor dead! An' they had to pick 'im up and shake 'im alive again"[22]

The complete identification of the enslaved with the trickster character, however, is somewhat problematic. Levine writes, "The problem with the notion that slaves completely identified with the . . . trickster hero whose exploits were really protest tales in disguise is that it ignores much of the complexity and ambiguity inherent in these tales."[23] The trickster's methods to achieve success were often deceitful and sometimes brutal, such as in the above tale. Representations of the trickster in the collective histories of enslavement are fraught with contradiction. A certain tension exists in the tales concerning the question of whether they want their audience to celebrate the actions of the trickster or treat him with suspicion and caution. In the story recounted above, the audience may have granted Jim's behavior a sly smile, yet his fellow slaves eventually condemned his actions and informed the master of his antics because they were tired of him shirking the workload. Thus, representations of the trickster in the narratives of the formerly enslaved were certainly indefinite. The trickster's characteristics were both celebrated and deplored, his methods applauded yet appalling.

These tales should be understood as partially reflecting aspects of the world of the enslaved. The trickster was located within this world, where he represented a particular character that was both approved of and maligned. The tales narrated episodes of survival and success in important areas of enslaved men's life, such as in contests over food and women, but the methods of the trickster were exposed as underhanded and devious. The tales were intended to teach the enslaved about the possible nature of their competitors in significant areas of their lives and the ways in which they may have outwitted them. The ingenuity and cunning of the trickster usually meant that he was able to outsmart the strong and powerful who threatened him. Thus, on occasion, his character was also celebrated as an alternative identity that enslaved men might have sought to emulate, his behavior appearing to guarantee success in the arena of courtship and love. In one such story, Leon Berry recalled his uncle Jim, who tricked the patrollers night after night while he visited his girlfriend who lived on the other side of the river. Jim traveled by boat under the cover of darkness and thus lessened the risk of being caught. One night, however, it looked as if the patrollers had finally caught up with him. While he was sitting in his girlfriend's house talking the patrollers hollered in glee that they had finally "got him." Jim made his escape, however, courtesy of a little window. He subsequently "tore out down to the river, an' they go after 'im on with their horse but they couldn't catch him." In a moment of ultimate triumph, Jim sailed his boat out of the river and turned to the patrol gang shouting, "come and get me! . . . How Lord, I'll be back one night next week, but you won't catch me!" The patrollers never caught Jim and he continued to make his trips across the river to court his lover.[24]

The journeys that these enslaved men made to reach their loved ones were fraught with danger and posed numerous risks. To have known this and yet to still have made the effort expressed a deep commitment to the relationship in question. It also must have served to enhance the enslaved man's sense of himself as a man. The journey to their lover's door, in a metaphorical and literal sense, involved reclaiming positive aspects of a gender identity which within the context of slavery had largely been denied. "You have seen how a man was made a slave; you shall soon see how a slave was made a man."[25] In the physical, psychological, and metaphorical social spaces that courtship provided, the enslaved were able to reject and redefine prevailing white stereotypes concerning their gender identities and occupy a real sense of who they were as men and women.

Enslaved men cultivated the role of "provider" within their courtships, negotiating their ways around a system that sought to deny them this privilege. John Brickell suggests in his *History of North Carolina* that an informal economy had operated among the enslaved as early as the colonial period and that this economy was intimately linked to the processes of courtship. He wrote that slave men were provided "with a sufficient quantity of Tobacco for their own use, a part of which they may sell, and likewise on Sundays, they gather Snake–root . . . with this and the Tobacco they buy Hats and other Necessaries for themselves, *as Linen, Bracelets, Ribbons and several other Toys for their Wives and Mistresses."*[26] Many slaveholders were willing to provide their slaves a modicum of time in which they could develop the means to participate in the informal economy. John F. Thompkins, a physician and planter from North Carolina, stated that it was one of the rules of his plantation that the slaves be given "half of every Saturday, in order that they may have some time to keep their clothes clean and do work for themselves, as to get means to buy their tobacco, &c."[27] Other slaveholders preferred to integrate the ways in which the enslaved could participate in the informal economy into their daily work routines. This was the case with turpentine planter Benjamin Williams, who rewarded those who were willing to perform additional tasks such as cultivating pine trees.[28]

Despite the absence of the task system on the majority of North Carolinian plantations, many among the formerly enslaved recalled the possession of gardens or the performance of additional labor tasks in return for extra provisions as a fundamental aspect of their experiences of slavery.[29] Because the enslaved were expected to work for their owner from sunrise until dark, these plots were often cultivated during the evenings after a day's work. John Bectom remembered that his grandmother "plowed till dusk-dark before they left the fields to come to the house. . . . They gave the slaves an acre of ground to plant and they could sell the crop and have the money. The work on this acre was done on moooonshiny nights and holidays."[30] Similarly, Hannah Crasson, whose parents were enslaved in Wake County, recalled that her mother and father "worked their patches by moonlight; and worked for the white folks in the day time."[31]

The garden system exposed one of the central ironies that structured enslaved life during the antebellum period. They undoubtedly drew a sense of pride and achievement from the produce they cultivated on their own plots of land, which subsequently afforded them a degree of economic independence. Hannah Crasson proudly recalled that her father "made a barrel of rice every year."[32] Yet slaveholders also benefited from this arrangement. Not only did they believe that the cultivation of small plots of land engendered a sense of industry and enterprise in their slave workforce, but they also saw economic advantage to a system that resulted in their slaves supplementing the often meager rations of the plantation.

Slaveholders encouraged their slaves to participate in the informal economy and also maintained a degree of control over the way it was managed by purchasing their slaves' produce themselves. Chana Littlejohn, who was enslaved in Warren County, recalled that her master, Peter Mitchell, would purchase goods from his slave men. "Marster brought charcoal from de men which dey burnt at night an' on de holidays. Dey worked an' made de stuff, an' marster would let dem have de steercarts an' wagons to carry deir corn an' charcoal to sell it in town."[33] Similarly, Hannah Crasson recalled that her mother and father sold the rice that they made to their master.[34]

Within the collective memories of enslavement, participation in the informal economy was however recollected with pride. Enslaved men and women cultivated skills within their daily working lives, which they were then willing to appropriate in the context of their own private worlds, transforming them into meaningful acts for themselves, their families, and the wider enslaved community. John Blassingame argues that those men and women, who were able to service the needs of the enslaved community as a whole through their positions on the plantation, ranked top of the hierarchy that the enslaved created for themselves.[35] A cook willing to make extra provisions for her family, or a carpenter who took some extra wood to make furniture for his loved ones would have commanded a large degree of respect among the enslaved community as they helped to ensure its survival.

Tempie Herndon Durham remembered Mammy Rachel, who was based in the dyeing room of the plantation in Chatham County, and her immense knowledge and skills at her occupation: "Dey wuzn' nothin' she didn' know 'bout dyein'. She know every kind of root, bark, leaf an' berry dat made red, blue, green, or whatever color she wanted." For enslaved women based in these sorts of working environments it was a willing step they made to sew, knit, and create clothing for their families and the wider enslaved community. Anna Mitchell recalled that her mother was a seamstress for the slaveholder, Joseph Hargrove, in Vance County. She remembered the time and effort that her mother used to put into producing clothes for the enslaved: "I'se knowed her ter wuck all night an' half de day ter make clothes fer de slaves."[36] Betty Coffer recalled the enslaved woman on Dr. Beverly Jones's plantation in Wachovia who knitted all the stockings for his slaves. "I mind she had one finger all twisted an' stiff from holdin' her knittin' needles."[37]

Some of the enslaved chose to sell their products in the informal economy, physical testimonies of the skills that they possessed, so that their families would not do without. Hannah Plummer told her WPA interviewer that her enslaved mother, who was owned by Governor Manly in Wake County, used to make their bed clothes. "She also made bonnets and dresses. Sometimes she made bonnets and sold them."[38] Recall Hannah Crasson who had recounted that although her mother and father sold the rice they made to the master, she had added with a sense of pride that "He made a barrel of rice a year, my daddy did."[39] These men and women, recalled with such esteem and dignity by their kith and kin, must have been the very backbones of their households and families, desperately trying to hold them together despite the odds that were set against them; weaving, knitting, sewing, and laboring so that their families could at least maintain a sense of respect and self-worth.

Several of these recollections referred to the ways in which men would make practical use of their leisure time to provide material benefits for their loved ones. Of course, on the one hand such activity served to strengthen the slave system, as enslaved men supplemented plantation rations. The formerly enslaved Lunsford Lane made the point in his narrative that "I had in fact to support both my wife and children, while he [the slaveholder] claimed them as his property."[40] Yet, on the other hand, enslaved men could cultivate their roles as providers to their families and loved ones. Although the slaveholder may have interpreted such behavior as beneficial to themselves, they also could not have been unaware of the ways in which such actions changed the relationship of enslaved men to their kith and kin, and the roles that they assumed within their own households. Hunting or fishing was one of the measures enslaved men employed in order to supplement the standard rations of the plantation.[41] Giving gifts of food to a loved one is regarded in many cultures as an important ritual with various social meanings attached to this expression of love. Through the provision of food enslaved men were able to express their feelings for another, demonstrating their wish and capabilities to care and provide for them. Louisa Adams recalled that during slavery her mother and father had their own garden patches and hogs, which the family lived on. Her father also supplemented his family's diet by hunting. She explained that "My old daddy partly raised his chilluns on game. He caught rabbits, coons an' possums. He would work all day and hunt at night."[42] Similarly, John Smith recalled that the enslaved men on his plantation "caught rabbits in gums, birds in traps an' hunted possums wid dogs at night."[43]

By supplementing the rations of the plantation, in providing extra food for his loved ones even though it required working all day and night, enslaved man were able to assert an alternative masculine identity to that imposed upon them in the context of slavery. Nicolas Proctor argues that hunting was an index of masculinity at a relatively early age for enslaved men. Moreover, this activity took on much more significance as they entered adolescence and began to establish more personal and intimate relationships. The formerly enslaved Zeb Crowder, who was enslaved at Swift Creek, recalled how he used to share his portion of the game that he caught: "We briled 'em over coals o' fire and fried 'em in fryin' pans and sometimes we had a bird stew, wid all de birds we wanted."[44] By sharing their spoils, these men assumed the mantle of providers and in the process they consequently "challenged their owner's authority and refuted the often emasculating influence of slave society."[45]

The case of Lily, discussed in the opening vignette of this chapter, illustrates the ways in which Robert sought to protect her from the whippings that she received at the hands of her master and overseer. Although Lily was cast as the assertive character of their relationship, "[Robert] beg me not ter let my mouth be so sassy, but I can't help hit." He desperately tried to defend her, acting in the role of "protector," attempting to shield her from the most horrific aspects of the inhumane system under which they had been forced to live. Robert defended Lily after they had begun to court. However, other men would make courageous efforts to protect a woman to gain their favor. Laura Bell recalled how her father, Wesley, made his first impressions on her mother, Minerva Jane, on Mack Strickland's plantation near Mount Airy. She explained that "Marse Mack's overseer, I doan know his name, wus gwine ter whip my mammy onct, an' pappy do' he aint neber make no love ter mammy comes up an' takes de whuppin' fer her."[46] Wesley's gallant act established a courting relationship with Minerva Jane where they "cou'ts on Sadday an' Sunday an' at all de sociables till dey gits married."[47]

Inflicting whippings on recalcitrant female slaves was intended to strip enslaved women such as Minerva Jane and Lily of their sense of personhood—their sense of themselves as human beings, individuals, and women. Their subjection to a whipping served to reinforce the notion that they were not "real" women at all but rather animals or brutes in need of discipline and punishment. In the act of defending these women, Wesley and Robert had protected them from harm and helped them both to retain a degree of femininity. In taking a whipping for their lovers, these enslaved men were transforming themselves from "slave" to "protector," not only of their physical safety but also their sense of themselves as women, as people, as human beings.

Although slave women were defined in the minds of southern slaveholders as sexually promiscuous, several examples serve to illustrate the contrary, revealing instead their modest behavior in the courting relationship. Previous chapters have cited examples of women such as Lucy Ann Dunn and Laura Bell. These women established courting relationships in the immediate aftermath of emancipation. These relationships were governed by certain moral codes that prevented either of them acting on their sexual desire until after they were married. Laura Bell, for example, would not let Thomas kiss her until they were married. Jim waited a year before he asked Lucy Ann to marry him and even after such a length of time she recalled, "He aint kissed me yet."[48] Similarly, Barbara Haywood recalled in her narrative that although she had known Frank since she was a child, when they were both enslaved in Wake County, she was far too shy to communicate her feelings to him and she was forced to wait for Frank to initiate their relationship. She recalled that after the Civil War, she and her family moved to Raleigh, where, she explained, she was able to see Frank most days. "I went ter school a little at Saint Paul's. Frank was wurkin' at de City Market on Fayetteville Street an' I'd go seberal blocks out of my way mornin' an' night on my way ter school ter look at him."[49] It is possible to deduce from Barbara's behavior that she had not wanted to be too forward in her approach to Frank. In many ways, Barbara appeared to be acting upon a notion of feminine respectability and honor that dictated that she should wait for Frank to approach her rather than declare her own feelings first. Frank finally did make the first move; as Barbara explained, "I is thirteen so he comes ter see me an' fer a year we co'uts."[50]

The behavior of women such as Barbara belied the myths that had emerged out of the slaveholding South regarding slave women's sexual appetite and their promiscuity. While these examples are taken from the postemancipation period it is evident that these women and their parents carried a blueprint into freedom that stressed female respectability and honor. It is also evident that Frank Haywood had purposefully waited until Barbara was a certain age before he initiated their courtship, therefore revealing his own code of masculine morality. The images that emerge in these narratives thus directly contrast with contemporary white representations of slave men as sexually threatening and governed by their libidos. When Lily Perry discussed Robert's marriage proposal to her, shortly after emancipation, she emphasized his humility and modesty. Lily explained that "We wus at a frolic at Louisburg when he proposes ter me an' he do hit dis way, Honey gal, I knows dat you doan love me so powerful much, but will you try ter do it fer me?" In response to his proposal she declared, "iffen I doan love yo' den dar ain't no water in Tar riber."[51] Similarly, Frank's proposal to Barbara Haywood was characterized by a sense of shyness and reticence. She recalled that "We wus sittin' in de kitchen at de house on Davis Street when he axes me ter have him an' I has him. I knows dat he tol' me dat he warn't worthy but dat he loved me an' dat he'd do anything he could ter please me, an' dat he'd always be good ter me."[52] Far removed from white images of the sexually menacing and aggressive black male, the men in these narratives were defined as both unassuming and modest in the context of a relationship that was intimately connected to sexual desire.

The enslaved also elucidated upon idealized gender identities through their folklore tales, which communicated, in particular, the ways in which enslaved men expected women to behave in the context of a courtship. In the context of West African societies, argues Mineke Schipper, the gender of the narrator of the folklore tale has a profound effect on the representations of men and women contained in the narratives. She suggests that in those tales that were related by men, women were generally depicted negatively and the stories acted as a warning to men that they must continuously protect themselves and their property against the intentions of their wife.[53] The construction of gender differences in these folklore tales represents for Schipper an attempt to veil the ideological power struggles in which one party benefits from the preservation of existing differences, and the other constantly seeks to reduce them. "These conflicting interests are expressed in the different ways in which male and female authors tell the same story from oral tradition."[54]

Enslaved understandings of courtship, as expressed in these tales, suggest that some aspects of enslaved ideals were the products of enslavement in the New World and the cultural interaction between blacks and whites in antebellum America. Other aspects of the tales also suggest that the enslaved were aware of and responded to changing ideals concerning love, courtship, and marriage on the North American mainland.[55] In particular, female choice is often woven into the tales, usually in contrast to their patriarchal features, such as the male authority figure. In one such tale concerning a corn shucking competition between Brer Rabbit and Brer Coon to win the hand of Miss Wolf, the final decision and resolution of the competition rests with Miss Wolf. Brer Rabbit had his heart set on winning the hand of Miss Wolf yet knew he was unable to compete with Brer Coon at shucking corn. Rather than spending his time trying to shuck the most corn, Brer Rabbit sang, danced, and charmed Miss Wolf while the others were engaged in the corn shucking. At the end of the contest, Brer Rabbit declared himself the winner, and Brer Wolf left the decision of who was to be crowned victorious to his daughter. Brer Rabbit's attempts at wooing Miss Wolf were successful, and she declared, "[I]t most surely are Brer Rabbits pile."[56]

At the heart of this fable lies the issue of male rivalry and the conflict and competition that courtship could entail. The two characters possessed very different skills. Brer Coon was a hard worker, known for his ability to work well and shuck corn. These features were highly prized in the animal kingdom as they helped ensure survival through the provision of food. In offering his daughter to the hardest worker Brer Wolf defined the qualities that an enslaved father might have desired in a suitor for his daughter: someone willing to work to provide for her. However, Brer Rabbit's character realized the futility of hard work for it was not the worker that Miss Wolf sought but the lover. Brer Rabbit was a charmer, and it was this characteristic that took Miss Wolf's fancy. In declaring Brer Rabbit the winner, Miss Wolf's gullible nature is revealed to the audience. Brer Rabbit had cheated in the contest; his "dancing and singing plum turned Miss Wolf's head."[57] She promptly based her decision on Brer Rabbit's romantic attributes of charm and style rather than on concern for her own future practical needs. At the corn shucking, Brer Rabbit rejected the work that was demanded of him, and this in part may have been what attracted Miss Wolf. Unlike enslaved men and women in reality, and Brer Coon in the tale, who had been forced to incorporate their courting lives into the world of work, Brer Rabbit rejected the labor and focused his attentions on winning the woman in question.

Likewise, in "Brother Rabbit's Courtship," Brer Rabbit found himself hopelessly in love with a girl who refused to marry anybody until she received some sort of sign; thus Brer Rabbit resolved to win her heart through trickery and deceit. Using the girl's revelation, Brer Rabbit laid his plans and provided her with a sign by means of a so-called secret singer, who told her that she would see her beau down by the big pine. When the girl next visited the big pine, there was Brer Rabbit waiting for her to arrive. "Dey jawered 'roun' a right smart, en 'spute 'long wid one 'n'er. But Brer Rabbit, he got de gal."[58] Neither female character is represented as having chosen wisely in Brer Rabbit as a suitor. He is a trickster, who cheated them of their affections and would probably fail to provide for them in the future. Yet, the possibility of female choice in both these tales needs to be underlined. Such themes undoubtedly reflect a shift within North American society more generally toward companionate marriage and declining parental influence and suggest that the enslaved were aware of, and were responding to, such changes within their own social and personal worlds.

Despite the prerogative of choice given to certain female characters in the courtship tales, representations of femininity and female characteristics are ambiguous in the stories. In the majority of courtship tales, women are cast as trophies in the contests between the male competitors or as passive members of the audience. In the tales where choice is awarded to women—such as in the corn shucking contest—the women are revealed to the audience as foolish and romantic who have selected their future spouses on the basis of highly unrealistic ideals. Female characters are thus often defined in the tales as stupid, naïve, and foolish, especially in relation to the trickster. However, in those tales where they assume the main role, they are usually represented as wicked and spiteful in nature. These undesirable qualities form the basis of the tale, which unfolds to the detriment of the female character.

In comparison to Brer Rabbit's self-confident manner, which usually results in his success in the courtship arena, female pride and vanity are often ridiculed by a trickster taking advantage of these traits. In the story "Why Brother Bull Growls and Grumbles," Brer Bull changed himself into a man and began courting a woman. Brer Bull's affections had such an affect on the woman that she could "skacely cook dinner. . . . She can't keep 'way fum de lookin'glass, a-breshin 'er ha'r en plasterin' down her beau-ketchers."[59] Her vanity, caused by Brer Bull's affection, can be seen to cloud her judgment, and it was only because of the little boy who lived with her that the true identity of her lover was revealed: "He notice dat when de man wuz courtin', dey wan't no Brer Bull in de pastur, en when dey wan't no man er courtin', dar wuz Brer Bull grazin' roun'."[60] The woman of the story was so flattered by her lover's attention that she had failed to notice the nature of his true character. Hence, the story suggests the effects that courtship could have on women, turning them into vain fools.

Interestingly, vanity is manifest by neglecting practical, domestic duties such as cooking dinner in favor of self-indulgent activities such as looking in the mirror and brushing one's hair. Female vanity is presented negatively in the tales, as a trait that disrupts the domestic harmony of the household. These attitudes reveal a great deal about gender roles and expectations among the enslaved. Although enslaved women labored in the field and performed domestic work for their master and mistress, they also carried out household duties for their own family.[61] As the tales suggest, domestic skills were highly desirable among enslaved women, and the stories narrate the possible fate of those who choose to neglect such important "womanly" duties.

In a similar story, "The Little Boy and His Dogs," a woman's vanity hampered her ability to care properly for her children. In the tale, two panthers, dressed as women, visit the home of a little boy and his mother. She is so impressed by their clothes and manners that she panders to their every need, ignoring the little boy's doubts about their identity. When he exclaimed to his mother that the two ladies were lapping water she responded, "I recken dat's de way de quality folks does, honey." When the little boy again asked his mother what she thought because they have "got little bit er hairy han's en arms" she again remarked, "I recken all de quality folks is got um, honey." The mother is so impressed by the ladies' finery that she ignored her little boy's observations and demanded that he show the two women the way down the road. Once they were far away from the boy's house the panthers revealed their true identities. His two faithful dogs, Minnyminny Morack and Follerlinsko, eventually saved him. At the end of the tale his mother learned by her mistakes and declared that "she ain't never gwine ter set no sto' by folks wid fine cloze, kaze dey so 'ceitful; no, never, so long as de Lord mout spar'er."[62]

Folkloric understandings of vanity and pride and their consequences are presented with humor in these tales, and the audience is encouraged to ridicule the vain woman who fell in love with a bull or the proud mother whose child was nearly eaten by panthers. These feminine characteristics are criticized in the tales but are not represented as dangerous or threatening to enslaved men in the context of forming a courtship. Indeed, in several of the courtship contests, the trickster exploits these particular feminine characteristics to win the young woman's attention and affections. The tales seem to suggest that women with such characteristics are easy targets for the unreliable, cheating trickster. The women in the above stories are cast as foolish rather than corrupt, but in other tales female characters are presented as evil. These women usually had some form of magical power that they used to do harm, especially to men. A common character in such stories is the witch, who slipped her skin or transformed herself as a disguise so that she might trick her intended victim. Usually the witch was depicted as some sort of animal. For example, in "Uncle Remus's Wonder Story," the witch changed itself into a woman when it was hungry in order to court an unsuspecting man, marry him, and then eat him.[63] Similarly, in the story of the "Man and the Wild Cattle," a young white calf transformed itself into a beautiful young woman. Her task was to trick the hunter to fall in love with her and eventually create a circumstance where the herd might kill him.[64]

It is interesting to note that in both tales, the narratives unfold in the context of courtship. These characters had to entrap men through love before their wicked designs could be carried out. The witch must court a man before it can satisfy its hunger and eat him, while the calf married the hunter to kill him. As in all the courtship contests narrated in the tales, these two illustrate the ways in which love can fall victim to external factors, including trickery, deceit, and bad magic. Yet, Brer Rabbit always retains a degree of likeability about him, no matter what depths he sank to outwit his rival; the women discussed above, who occupy the role of trickster, have no positive attributes and are instead represented as inherently wicked. Within these tales then the central concern appears to be the dangers of assertive female sexuality. The female characters in both these stories are cast in the leading role, yet their power over the courtship is defined as dangerous and disrupting. Such ideas within the enslaved community regarding female sexuality might be compared to the image of the so-called Jezebel, imposed upon slaves by their white masters and mistresses. Even though the enslaved did not share in these stereotypical characterizations of slave women, these folktales demonstrate that the enslaved too considered female sexual agency a dangerous and potentially disruptive force.

In the courtship contests involving Brer Rabbit, courting was carried out along specifically gendered lines and conformed to a particular pattern in which the male characters occupied active, assertive roles. The stories illustrate how the courtship of a couple should be carried out and the specific positions of the man and the woman within this process. In the contest over King Deer's daughter, for example, Brer Rabbit, "[s]tidder scollopin' 'roun' en bowin' en scrapin', dey des go right straight atter de gal."[65] In turn, female characters often occupied a more passive position, allowing men to court them rather than being active agents of the relationship. In the folktales, as in reality, enslaved men took the lead role in courtship, and enslaved women usually took the more passive role. The tales in which female characters took an active control of a courtship therefore demonstrate the power of female sexuality and hint at the perceived threat that this posed to the established gender hierarchy. In the course of these tales, female empowerment in the courting relationship always resulted in their downfall and the end of the courtship. These tales therefore confirm accepted understandings of the role of men and women within the personal worlds of the enslaved and suggest that a reversal of these accepted gender roles and identities would ultimately lead to chaos, conflict, and confusion.

The romantic relationships of the enslaved, then, took place in spaces and places where the enslaved felt able to cut the shackles of slavery, embrace alternative identities, and communicate various understandings of courtship and love, as individual men and women, as protectors and providers, as lovers and romancers, as human beings. Within the landscapes of courtship that the enslaved created and called their own they were able to reject and redefine ideas concerning their sexual identity and the gendered dimensions of enslaved life. Such action gave voice to the lies of slavery which proclaimed that slaves were incapable of creating loving and meaningful relationships with one another.

The murder of one's master in order to preserve intimate ties was perhaps the most direct way in which this lie could be dismantled. Killing one's slaveholder in the name of love seems to have been as good a reason as any for some among the enslaved in the American South. In 1850, a fourteen-year-old girl named Celia was bought as the property of Robert Newsom, a prosperous landowner from Missouri. After enduring five years of sexual abuse and exploitation under his tyranny and having borne him two children in the process, she subsequently murdered him in 1855 after he threatened her intimate relationship with George, an enslaved man from the neighborhood.[66] In Washington County, North Carolina, the Pettigrew Family papers document the murder of a local slaveholder, William Davenport, which provoked a range of responses among local inhabitants. Davenport was reportedly shot in February 1858 by three of his slaves. Gauzey, the enslaved man who was eventually incriminated for Davenport's murder was allegedly upset because "his master would not allow him to have a wife off and said he must 'fix things so that he could come and go.'"[67] Frustrated and no doubt angry at his master's refusal to let him manage his own emotional affairs, Gauzey evidently felt aggrieved enough to take drastic action. His options were limited, and in the often aggressive cultures of the antebellum slaveholding world it is perhaps not surprising that Gauzey resorted to the measures that he did.

Local whites reacted to the murder of Davenport with indignation, shock, and fear. For slaves to have acted in such a confrontational and assertive manner illustrated not only the possibilities for violent resistance from among the growing numbers of the enslaved in the state but also served to expose the lie that the white slaveholding master was in all ways powerful. Writing from one of the Pettigrew plantations on Lake Scuppernong, Jane North reported to her sister that the incident was "the first murder of this description ever known in this county & fills everybody with horror."[68] The *horror* Jane North described was that this event confirmed in her eyes the worst fears of the local slaveholding population; that the enslaved were a potentially threatening and dangerous force.

Similar tales of cruel slaveholders meeting a sudden and grisly end at the hands of desperate couples are a common theme in the vernacular histories of enslavement. Dave Lawson related the story of his grandparents, Cleve and Lissa, who killed their master, Drew Norwood, after Cleve became aware of Norwood's desire to sell Lissa. "Cleve 'gun to sweat. He turned so sick an' skeered dat he could hardly swing de scythe through de wheat. Marse Drew done took his baby away, an' now sumpin' way down in his heart tole him dat he was gwine take Lissa."[69]

The story Dave Lawson recollected is worth quoting at length for it extrapolates on the twisted and perverse strands of power and resistance that structured the southern slave system:

> When 'twuz good an' dark Cleve took a long rope an' went out tellin' Lissa to keep de water boilin'. When he come back he had Marse Drew all tied up wid de rope an' gagged so he couldn' holler; he had him th'owed over his shoulder like a sack of meal. He brung him in de cabin an' laid him on de floor, den he tole him if he wouldn' sell Lissa dat he wouldn' hurt him. But Marse Drew shook his head an' cussed in his th'oat. Den Cleve took off de gag, but befo' de white man could holler out, Cleve stuffed de spout of a funnel in his big mouf way down his th'oat, holdin' down his tounge. He ax him one more time to save Lissa from de block, but Marse Drew look at him wid hate in his eyes shook his head again. Cleve didn' say nothin' else to him; he call Lissa an' tole her to bring him a pitcher of boilin' water.[70]

The murder of Drew Norwood underlines the desperate and heart-wrenching situation that many enslaved couples across the South must have faced, tortured by the fear of sale and the prospect of never seeing one another again. The action taken by Lissa and Cleve illustrates the extreme measures that enslaved couples were sometimes forced to employ in their frantic attempts to remain together. For most this prospect must have felt like a virtual death. While we do not know the actual fate of Gauzey, it is evident that he was indicted for the murder of Davenport.[71] No doubt, he met a similar fate to that of Cleve and Lissa Lawson, who were hung with the very rope that they used to kill Norwood.

Overt acts of resistance such as these examples struck at the heart of southern white society, and punishment was usually swift and particularly brutal. In their resistance against their master, Cleve and Lissa Lawson had paid a heavy price. Yet in a certain respect, they had managed to defy the ultimate control exercised by the slaveholder, for they were not separated, not even in death. As Dave Lawson recounted, "Sometimes now in de fall of de year when I'se settin' in de door after de sun done gone down; an' de wheat am ripe an' bendin' in de win', an' de moon am roun' an yeller like a mush melon, seems like I sees two shadows swingin' from de big lim' of dat tree—I sees dem swingin' low side by side wid dey feets near 'bout touchin' de grou'."[72]

Of course, Dave Lawson's account of Cleve and Lissa may not have been entirely factual, and it was almost certainly embellished to serve the craft of storytelling.[73] However, while we may question the reliability of Dave Lawson's account, its real value lies in the meanings that such a tale may have conveyed. Whether it was an authentic reflection of events was not the point of the story. Instead, the tale was intended to underline the strength and intensity of the ties that bound enslaved couples together and the brutalities of the slave system that attempted to drive them apart. The image described by Dave Lawson of the ghosts of Cleve and Lissa hanging from the limb of the tree served to provide a haunting and persistent reminder during the 1930s that these people had once existed, that they had laughed and cried; felt joy and sorrow, fear and comfort. Most important, they had loved and been loved.

Much like Alonzo Haywood's evaluation of his parent's relationship cited in the Introduction, Dave Lawson's account of Lissa and Cleve suggests that there was an enduring belief among the formerly enslaved of the strength and sincerity of love between enslaved couples. In the narrative of Dave Lawson, Cleve and Lissa's love was so strong that it had held them together in death, as it had done in life. Enslaved love was certainly nothing to have poured scorn upon.

5

A Red Satin Ribbon Tied around My Finger
The Meaning of the Wedding Ceremony

RECALLING HER marriage to Exter, an enslaved man who resided on a neighboring plantation in Chatham County, Tempie Herndon Durham brought to mind the moments of the day that she and Exter had enjoyed: "When I growed up I married Exter Durham. He belonged to Marse Snipes Durham who had de plantation 'cross de county line in Orange County. We had a big weddin'. We was married on de front po'ch of de big house. Marse George killed a shoat an' Mis' Betsy had Georgianna, de cook, to bake a big weddin' cake all iced up as white as snow wid a bride an' groom standin' in de middle holdin' han's." Through Tempie's reminiscences she communicated to her interviewer the ways in which she and Exter had reclaimed the event for themselves, transcending the status of slaves and embracing the alternative identities of bride and groom:

> Dat was some weddin'. I had on a white dress, white shoes an' long white gloves dat come to my elbow, an' Mis' Betsy done made me a weddin' veil out of a white net window curtain. When she played de weddin' ma'ch on de piano, me an' Exter ma'ched down de walk an' up on de po'ch to de altar Mis' Betsy done fixed. Dat de pretties' altar I ever seed. Back 'gainst de rose vine dat was full of red roses, Mis' Betsy done put tables filled wid flowers an' white candles. She done spread down a bed sheet, a sho nuff linen sheet, for us to stan' on, an' dey was a white pillow to kneel down on. Exter done made me a weddin' ring. He made it out of a big red button wid his pocket knife. He done cut it so roun' an' polished it so smooth dat it looked like a red satin ribbon tide 'roun' my finger.[1]

The significance of this type of wedding day for the enslaved should not be underplayed. Indeed, Graham and Shane White argue that their reading of the WPA narratives suggests that the ritual of the wedding "may well have been the point when slave behavior on antebellum plantations most nearly corresponds to that of whites."[2]

In particular, they cite examples of enslaved women who on their wedding days dressed in white gowns that were cast-offs from their mistress. The dresses were usually then adapted by the addition of bows or sashes as with Tempie's wedding veil, which had been adapted from an old net curtain owned by her mistress. Similarly, in the narrative of Sally Williams, who was enslaved in Fayetteville, her own wedding dress was a cast-off from her mistress, to which she then added "a bright ribbon for her waist and a gauze handkerchief to tie around her head." She described the groom, Abram, as "equally destitute," and thus he obtained some hand-me-down clothes from his master "which made him look, so Sally thought, quite like a gentleman."[3] Alice Baugh, in recalling the story of her parents' wedding day remembered that her mother "w'ar Miss Mary's weddin' dress, all uv white lace, an' dat my pappy w'ar Mr. Charlie's weddin' suit wid a flower in de button hole."[4] Enslaved men and women from across the South recalled how they appropriated and altered the wedding attire of their masters and mistresses in order that they could use it for their own ceremony. Ellen Betts, who was enslaved in Texas, recalled that after her master had married 'Miss Cornelia' "de nex' day she give her weddin' dress to my ma. Dat de fines' dress I ever seen. It was purple and green silk and all de nigger gals wear dat dress when dey marry."[5]

In addition to reclaiming the event for themselves, enslaved couples such as Tempie and Exter were also partaking in an act that served symbolic functions for the wider enslaved community as a whole. These wedding ceremonies should be understood as a very public confirmation that the enslaved refused the system of slavery and its trade in human beings. They refused a system that forced the separation of loving and devoted couples. They refused a system that denied them the legal right to marry and establish their own households. They refused a system that at its very heart defined them as property, to be bought and sold at will. Living under a system aimed to crush their individuality and cripple their emotional capacities, the enslaved, through the ritual of the wedding ceremony, were offering one of the most complex and multifaceted acts of resistance to the system as a whole.

The wedding ceremonies of the enslaved were typically conducted by the slaveholder and were often symbolized through acts such as jumping the broomstick. Ophelia Whitley remembered that "[w]hen de slaves got married dey done it dis way: de marster hilt a broom an' dey solemnly steps over it twict den dey kiss and dey wuz married, 'course dar was something dat de marster said, but I done forgot what it wuz."[6] Willie Cozart of Zebulon in Wake County, related in his interview with the WPA that the man had to ask the master before he could marry the woman, "an he jest tol' dem to step ober de broom an' dat wuz de way de got married dem days."[7] John Bectom also recalled that "[t]he marsters married the slaves without any papers. All they did was to say . . . 'Frank, I pronounce you and Jane man and wife'"[8]

Formerly enslaved men and women from other slaveholding states recalled these types of wedding ceremonies during slavery. George Womble, enslaved in Georgia, remembered that when enslaved couples were married "the master . . .

asked each in turn if they wished to be joined as man and wife and if both answered that they did they were taken into the master's house where the ceremony would be conducted." He further confirmed that the couple would participate in a broomstick ceremony, where afterward they would be pronounced as husband and wife.[9] Delia Briscoe recalled that courtships were extremely brief and once the relationship had been reported to the master, courtesy of an elderly man he employed to watch what went on in the slave quarters, the master would then question the couple "and if they consented, were married without the benefit of clergy."[10] John White from Oklahoma recalled that his pappy and mammy were married by the master. Mary, his mammy, had insisted that "a preacher wedding is best." Her protests, however, were to no avail. "Master says he can marry them just as good. There wasn't no bible. Just an old Almanac. Master White read something out of that. That's all and they was married. The wedding was over!"[11]

The lack of recognition that some slaveholders gave to the marital relations of their slaves was justified in their own eyes through the fact that these were not legal unions—as property slaves could not lawfully enter into any form of contract, including that of marriage. However, there were some slaveholders who were willing to provide their slaves with more of a ceremonial start to their married life. Indeed, in some cases it necessitated the enslaved couple having to challenge their master and mistress for ownership of the day. The presence of "Marse George" and "Mis' Betsy," for example, haunts Tempie Herndon Durham's account of her wedding day. Similarly, Alice Baugh's recollections of her parents' wedding day revealed in the telling that the most prominent actors in this social performance were the master and mistress. As well as her mammy and pappy wearing cast-offs from the wardrobes of "master Charlie" and "Missus Mary," she also recounted that they "give a big dance atter de supper dey had, an' master Charlie dance de fust set wid my mammy."[12]

The legal and physical claims that these slaveholders had over their slaves had ostensibly extended into the ownership of their emotional lives too. Women such as Miss Betsy, it seemed, had been enveloped by the rhetoric of love and romance that was popular within her own social class. At the wedding of a favored domestic such as Tempie, Miss Betsy saw an opportunity for herself to partake in these specific representations of romantic love. The irony of Miss Betsy's actions was most clearly illustrated when Tempie referred to the end of the day, when she and Exter retired to their cabin together. "After de weddin' we went down to de cabin Mis' Betsy done all dressed up, but Exter couldn' stay no longer dat night kaze he belonged to Marse Snipes Durham an' he had to back home."[13] Their condition as slaves prevented them from living together as husband and wife, and Miss Betsy, as Tempie's mistress, was wholly compliant with this situation. However, she had also provided a wedding day for Tempie and Exter predicated around idealized notion of the married couple living as husband and wife, happily ever after.

Tempie's recollection of her wedding revealed the limits that were placed on and around enslaved life and the stake that many slaveholders had in controlling the emotional lives of their slaves. Tempie had mentioned Exter's gift to her of a ring, which he had given her during the wedding service. She recalled with a sense of pride that "[h]e made it out of a big red button wid his pocket knife. He done cut it so roun' an' polished it so smooth dat it looked like a red satin ribbon tide 'roun' my finger." She also related to her interviewer that she wore the ring for fifty years; however, "den it got so thin dat I lost it one day in de wash tub when I was washin' clothes."[14] Through his own skills and workmanship, Exter had transformed the *big red button* into a *red satin ribbon* that had remained on Tempie's finger for fifty years. She had also worn a white dress with matching shoes and with gloves that had come up to her elbows, dressed in her finery in order to make the day feel that extra bit special.

However, looked at from another perspective, the satin red ribbon was in reality a red button that had eventually worn away. Tempie's white gown, gloves, and shoes were complimented by a makeshift veil made from an old net curtain that her mistress no longer needed. These aspects of Tempie's wedding day seem particularly stark when considered against the backdrop of the idealized romantic images that also accompany her narrative, such as the flowers, white candles, and wedding cake. They served to underline the complexities of mastery in the old South, the ways in which ownership was expressed, and the extent of these claims. In turn, enslaved men and women such as Exter and Tempie refused the scope of these terms of ownership and sought to appropriate and transform the meanings that slaveholders such as "Marse George" and "Miss Betsy" had provided for them.

It was not just about the clothing that they wore or the gifts that were exchanged. It was also about the ceremony itself—who was present and, perhaps more important, who presided over it. Julius Nelson recalled that on the plantation in Anson County where he had been enslaved, Master Nelson used to provide his slaves with a *"regular weddin' wid a preacher* an' all de fixin's an de marster usually gave us a big supper." He further remarked that the reason for the master's hospitality toward his slaves was that he would be provided with more slaves as a result of this union.[15] The formerly enslaved Richard Moring remarked on the weddings that had occurred between enslaved men and women on the plantation of his master in Wake County, stating that "[w]hen dere was a weddin' dar wus fun fer all, case hit wus a big affair. Dey wus all dressed up in new clothes, an' marster's dinin' room wus decorated wid flowers fer de 'casion. De ban' which wus banjos, an fiddles 'ud play an' de neighborin' folk 'ud come. *De preacher married 'em up good an' tight just lak he done de white folks.* An atter hit wus ober an' de songs wus sung marsters dinn' table wus set an' dar wus a weddin' supper fer all."[16] Anna Wright declared that the weddings on the plantation in Scotland County during slavery days were "somethin' fine. . . . De niggers dressed lak a white folks weddin' an' de circuit person married dem in de big house parlour. . . . Atter de ceremony wus over dar'd be a feas' an' a dance."[17]

It is evident from statements such as these that the presence of the preacher at the wedding ceremonies of the enslaved fundamentally changed the meaning of the occasion. Such occasions were mediated by the enslaved in order that they might negotiate their desire for their own zones of emotional autonomy. Enslaved cultural practices may have appropriated some elements of the white slaveholding elite in their wedding ceremonies—the type of dress they wore, the gifts they exchanged, and the person who married them, for example. Nevertheless, they also sought to claim this day as their own, and they made small but extremely significant additions to their ceremony so that this objective might be achieved.

For the slaveholder at least, enslaved couples could never be married up *good and tight just like the white folk*, because they were always subject to sale and separation, either through the slaveholder's desire for further profit, estate division following death or dowry, or simply their own precarious whims. Yet, the enslaved used influences such as the preacher to provide more recognition of their marital ties and thus create some sort of stability and security in their own eyes. Because only a small number of enslaved couples enjoyed the privilege of a preacher overseeing their marriage ceremony, this more official marriage ceremony may have forced the slaveholder to recognize the validity of the relationship. Consequently they may have been more reluctant to separate such couples through sale. The enslaved would not have been unaware of this and may in part have sought to sanction their union through the preacher for this very reason. In addition, it is evident that couples who participated in the ritual of a wedding ceremony also had an immense sense of pride if a preacher had married them. Enslaved couples would have gained strength and support from the messages conveyed by the preacher, a sense of hope that in spite of everything they would survive the traumatic ordeal of slavery together. Tempie recollected that when she married Exter "Uncle Edmond Kirby married us. He was de nigger preacher dat preached at de plantation church. After Uncle Edmond said de las' words over me an' Exter, Marse George got to have his little fun. He say, come on Exter, you an' Tempie got to jump over de broomstick backwards; you got to do dat to see which one gwine be boss of your househol'."[18]

Tempie's narrative indicates that the preacher's blessing signified something more tangible in comparison to the more customary slave tradition of jumping the broomstick. She objected to the broomstick wedding, describing it as *her master's fun* and instead stressed the presence of the preacher, possibly because he represented the authority of God as compared to the authority of Master

George. Similarly, Anna Wright, mentioned above, had recalled that the circuit parson married enslaved couples in the parlor of the big house where her mother had been enslaved in Scotland County. However, in contrast to Tempie Herndon Durham's master, who seemed to somewhat dismiss the significance of the religious aspect of their wedding, James Ellis, the master of Anna Wright's mother, was quite the opposite. She explained that "Mammy tol' me dat Marse James wus a very religious man, an' dat wus why de preacher married de slaves, an' why he made all of de slaves go ter church on Sunday an' say blessin' at meal times."[19]

It was usually favored domestic or skilled slaves who had the opportunity to be married by a preacher, reflecting the hierarchy imposed by the slaveholder. These were young couples rather than couples who had lived together for several years, reflecting the slaveholders' tacit assumption that these older couples were as good as married anyway and thus ensuring that the slaveholder need not be put to any more expense than was necessary. Resistance to the privileges afforded favored slaves during their marriage ceremonies was expressed in the aftermath of emancipation when, in 1866, nearly twenty thousand formerly enslaved men and women in North Carolina registered their marriages with county clerks and justices of the peace, each paying a fee of twenty five cents. This amounted to about 14 percent of North Carolina's entire adult population of enslaved men and women in 1860. A significant number of these marriages were recorded as having lasted over many years. In Halifax County, for example, 163 marriages were registered in 1866. Of these marriages, thirteen were between couples who had been together for more than thirty years and thirty-three for more than twenty years.[20] Others went a step further and sought validation by Protestant preachers, reflecting Rena Raines's attitude that "Mother and father come ter Raleigh atter de suurender an' wus married right."[21] Nevertheless, alternative scholarly arguments suggest that the enslaved did in fact regard their marriages as legal and binding during slavery and subsequently refused to reregister their unions in the aftermath of freedom. Leslie Schwalm argues that many formerly enslaved couples did not seek to register their marriages at the point of emancipation, having already affirmed their commitment to one another on a very public stage through a marriage ceremony conducted during slavery.[22]

Although white ministers would occasionally preside over the wedding ceremonies of the enslaved, the majority of preachers that oversaw enslaved weddings were African Americans. When performing such duties, white preachers were largely dismissive of enslaved couples and the meaning of the marriage ceremony to them. When Sidney Bumpas, a Methodist minister based in Raleigh, wrote to his wife concerning the wedding ceremonies he had recently conducted, he emphasized the ceremony of a white couple, Dr. Mason and Miss Hicks, describing the clothing and festivities in detail, "the doctor appeared in his common dress blue ____ and pantaloons and black vest . . . the party was small and no foolish plays were introduced." In contrast, the marriage between an enslaved man and woman is simply described as a union between "a couple of Negroes."[23]

No doubt, African American preachers were purposefully selected by the slaveholder for the job of presiding over these ceremonies. The African American preacher's function at such weddings was, in the eyes of the slaveholder, a convenient ruse serving to pacify the couple in question and the wider slave community while ensuring that the authority of the preacher could not question that of the slaveholder, should they later decide to separate a married couple through sale. However, the enslaved would have preferred an African American preacher presiding over their wedding ceremonies. Such preachers confirmed the link between the couple themselves and the wider enslaved community, as they selected sermons, prayers, and songs from which the enslaved derived significance and special meaning.

For example, Sally Williams, in her description of her wedding to Abram, stressed the religious service itself and the sermon of the preacher:

> The hour came, and with their bridesmaid and groomsman they stood up before the colored Methodist preacher who was in waiting. He opened the Bible and read the account of the marriage at Cana. Sally had never heard it before, and the thought that Jesus had been present at an earthly wedding, impressed her, more than anything had ever done, with the importance of what she was about to do . . . now an awe crept over her; she felt as if God were there, and resolved, in heart, to do all in her power for her new-found friend. The reading was followed by a prayer, and then they were pronounced husband and wife. There was a momentary hush in the room. All seemed touched by the services.[24]

For the enslaved, the significance of an African American preacher was fundamental to their marriage ceremonies because he incorporated extra meaning into these occasions. His presence symbolized that these unions were sanctified under the authority of God. The African American preacher represented the high moral standards of community life for the enslaved, confirming that they were far removed from the images of sexual licentiousness and uncivilized heathenism that white southerners had constructed and imposed upon them. For enslaved couples such as Sally and Abram, and Tempie and Exter, the authority of God was much more concrete and meant much more than the authority of their master and mistress.

Moreover, the preacher also voiced community sanctions for these unions and emphasized the fact that these communities would be expected to support the couple through the best and the worst of times: the birth of a baby, the death of a spouse, the building of a family home, the sale and separation from a loved one. While the slaveholder possessed the rights to sell them away from each other, thus making null and void the notion of "till death do us part," the validation of their union at God's altar and the approval of the wider enslaved community allowed for enslaved couples to confirm their love for each other in the most respectable and celebrated form possible.

The elements of the day which Tempie chose to stress, in addition to the preacher, were especially linked to a particular romanticized ideal: the white wedding dress, the wedding veil, red roses, and linen sheets. Enslaved women such as Tempie embraced the opportunity to not only confer some validity on their marital unions but also to provide it with authenticity and a respectability, *a wedding just like the white folks,* through those elements such as the wedding dress, the red roses, and, of course, the preacher. The preacher's role was not just to validate a nonlegal union for the enslaved. His presence was not just perfunctory or practical. It confirmed and authenticated a symbolic and significant rite of passage in the lives of the enslaved.

The importance of ritual at enslaved weddings is revealed through Tempie's various references to the dress, the flowers, and the quality of the material that functioned as Tempie and Exter's makeshift altar. John Gillis stresses the importance of ritual in the context of courtship and marriage, arguing that ritual is endemic in situations of change and at times of life when there is uncertainty. Accordingly, "Ceremony can make it appear that there is not conflict, only harmony, no disorder, only order, that if danger threatens, safe solutions are at hand."[25] For enslaved couples, always under the shadow of the threat of separation, the need to confirm and qualify their union through a showy ceremony, if given the opportunity, was hardly surprising.

Moreover, the ritual of the wedding ceremony itself, and the presence of the African American preacher in particular, were vital means to cultivate a heightened sense of respectability within the wider community. The marriage ceremony confirmed the shift in status to husband and wife for the couple concerned. It thus symbolized to the enslaved community the couple's commitment to each other and their pledge to the community as a whole. Through playing out their wedding ceremony in front of their friends and family and with all the accompanying ritual and festivities, these enslaved couples were ensuring that their marriage assumed a very public face, transforming a more private act into a public occasion. Gillis argues that the marriage ceremony represents a social drama in which not just the couple but several parties play crucial roles, including families, peers, and communities. Courtship and the marriage ceremonies of the enslaved created political dimensions and consequences for a network of individuals and the enslaved community at large. Through a public wedding, rather than a more informal ceremony, enslaved couples could engage the approval and support of the wider community. Thus, a big wedding ceremony presided over by a preacher served to confirm and strengthen extended familial ties as well as reinforcing the bonds of community for the enslaved.

Prior to their wedding ceremonies, the choice of partner for the enslaved was a complex process. Contrary to contemporary white southern opinion, the enslaved often went to great lengths to make themselves desirable to members of the opposite sex. Conversely, slaveholders worked strenuously to inscribe their authority on the body of the slave, most particularly through acts such as branding their skin and regulating their clothing.[26] Slaves were provided with an annual clothing allowance, usually during the Christmas period. This allowance typically consisted of standardized trousers and shirt for male slaves and dresses made from cheap calico fabric for females.[27] The slaveholder considered the clothing needs of the slave only in terms of work, thus there was little need for slave clothing to be made from fine colored fabrics or into attractive attire. Harriet Jacobs described the "linsey-woolsey dress" given to her each year by her mistress as "one of the badges of slavery."[28] It was not that the slaveholder failed to understand the significance of clothing for the enslaved. They were fully aware of the need to control the attire of their slave labor force. Through such regulation the slaveholder inscribed their rights of ownership on the physical body of the slave population and attempted to prevent the slave from expressing any individuality through their personal appearance.

The slaveholder was also able to use clothing as a means of disciplining the slave population. Lizzie Baker recollected that her mother, Teeny McLintire, who was enslaved in Duplin County, could not go to any dances during slavery because she was crippled. She related that this was the result of a punishment given to Teeny by her mistress. Lizzie explained that "a colored woman stole something when she wus hungry. She put it off on mother and missus made mother wear trousers for a year to punish her."[29] Teeny's mistress punished her by forcing her to wear male clothing, thus she not only had her slave "working like a man," but dressing like one too. In meting out this punishment, Teeny's mistress established the extent of her authority over the slaves that she owned. By dressing Teeny in men's clothing she underlined the very powerful and complex significance that clothing could represent, especially for the enslaved, who were struggling to affirm their identity on their own terms. The actions of Teeny's mistress forcefully underline the ways in which the slave's body and physical representation was used as a site of contestation and power. Several other examples exist from across the Americas that would suggest that, like Teeny's mistress, slaveholders used clothing as a means to punish and discipline their slaves. A Barbadian planter wrote in a letter during the 1830s that "in the case of one woman on my estate who had a more than ordinary fondness for pugilistic exercises, I made her put on a suit of her brother's clothes, that the habits might seem more becoming the sex. It had a good effect."[30] Similarly, Stephanie Camp cites an example taken from Octavia V. Rogers Albert's *The House of Bondage* of a woman named Nellie Johnson, enslaved in Louisiana, who was "forced to wear man's pants for one year."[31] The extract from the original source reveals that her owner "made her work in the field that way. . . . Aunt Jane said once while she was passing on the levee she saw Nellie working on the Mississippi River, and she had men's clothes on then."[32] These examples offer evidence that clothing was an integral part of the power dynamics shaping slave societies, most especially in relation to the negation of the gender identity of the enslaved by the white slaveholding classes.

Yet the enslaved did manage to reclaim a sense of autonomy over the clothing they wore. This was expressly so in the context of "Sunday clothing," which was obtained by the enslaved through extra labor they performed during their off-time. Graham and Shane White make the point that the major division in the slave dress code in the antebellum American South was not between different classes of the slaves but "between what individual slaves wore Monday through Saturday and what they wore on Sundays."[33] Sunday signified the day on which the majority of the enslaved were given a partial break from working and were allowed to engage in such activities as attending church, visiting loved ones, gardening, or simply resting. Hence, many of the enslaved, especially those who were attending Sunday Service or visiting loved ones, were dressed in their best clothing on this particular day.

The term Sunday clothing seemed to encompass all those clothes that were distinct from the standard plantation dress issued by the master and mistress, not just those reserved for Sundays in particular. Sunday clothing was worn during periods of social recreation and leisure by the enslaved and in social environments where they were most likely to socialize with members of the opposite sex. Henrietta McCullers recalled that on Sundays she and the other enslaved men and women on the plantation would follow her mistress's coach to church. "On Sundays you should o' seen us *in our Sunday bes'* goin' to church."[34] Enslaved men and women also recalled wearing their Sunday clothes at other special times too. Alice Baugh's mother recollected that during the Christmas holidays the enslaved were allowed a week's holiday, and she added, "dey had dere Sunday clothes, which wuz nice."[35]

Southern slaveholders generally concurred with their slaves' desire for Sunday clothing. H. N. McTyiere, in an essay for *De Bow's Review*, advised other slaveholders that it was a "commendable custom to furnish occasionally a Sunday or holiday attire" for their slaves for the purpose of cultivating a "proper self-respect" among them. It was also useful, he argued, in promoting "those associations that contribute to their moral improvement, and from which they would otherwise refrain."[36] Another slaveholder suggested that the only way to "cure a sloven [female slave]" was "to give her something nice occasionally to wear and praise her up to the skies whenever she has on anything tolerably decent."[37] Usually, however, slaveholders would refuse to go to any extra expense to obtain this extra clothing. One planter writing for *The American Cotton Planter and Soil of the South* suggested that the policy of southern planters toward their slaves should be that "[t]wo good suits of clothing a year shall be furnished them."

However, the author did allow his slaves a small piece of land to work so that they could supply themselves with their own Sunday suits.[38] Thus, the informal economy played a vital role in the realm of courtship. Reverend Francis Hawley, who spent fourteen years in the Carolinas, noted that he had never known an instance when the slaveholder put himself to any extra expense to provide his slaves with decent clothes. Yet he remarked, "If, by making baskets, brooms, mats, &c at night or on Sundays the slaves can get money enough to buy a Sunday suit, very well."[39]

Slaveholders were also concerned that their slaves present themselves respectably. Their cleanliness in dress spoke volumes about the slaveholders themselves and communicated to the wider white society how wealthy they were. An overseer on a South Carolina plantation advised slaveholders across the South to "[m]ake it a rule to oblige every negro to have his clothes mended as soon as you discover them broken." He advised that if the size of the labor force made it difficult to check every aspect of their dress, then the slaveholder should be persuaded to "have some old person to serve as a 'general mender' to the plantation, and you will never have to insult the eye with a set of ragged negroes."[40] One slaveholder listed in his *Model Rules for Plantation Governance* that "[t]he negroes are to appear in the *field* on Monday mornings cleanly clad." To facilitate their cleanliness he advised that they be allowed time on Saturday evenings to wash their clothes.[41]

The majority of slaveholders believed that their slaves were by nature filthy and without regard for personal hygiene or the state of their living quarters. Sarah Hicks Williams wrote to her parents complaining of her slaves' seemingly total disregard for maintaining their personal appearance. She wrote that "[a]t this season the women have each a thick dress, chemise, shoes and a blanket given them. The men pantaloons and jacket, shirt, blanket and shoes besides bonnet and caps. . . . [A]s a whole they are naturally filthy and it is discouraging to make for them, for it is soon in dirt and rags."[42] A Georgian physician writing an article for the *American Cotton Planter and Soil of the South* in 1860 concerning the "Peculiarities & Diseases of Negroes." declared that "[s]o notoriously filthy are negroes that many persons will doubtless smile at the very mention of cleanliness when used in connection with a people closely allied to hogs in their nature and habits."[43]

Despite slaveholder's claims to the contrary, however, the enslaved did take a great deal of care over their personal appearance. In fact, those visiting the southern states from the North often reflected upon this point. Sarah Hicks Williams had decided that her slaves were filthy by nature after she had settled into the role of slave mistress following a few months of marriage. However, when she had initially arrived in Greene County as a newlywed from New York in October 1853, her views were quite the reverse. She wrote of her incredulity at one of the field hands, who had asked her to ride over and get her a new dress from

"Snow Hill." One of the other slaves also requested that she "fix a dress for her." She also recounted that on Sundays the slaves would dress up and attend church. She declared that "many of them look very nice."[44] Thus before she became pervious to the common slaveholding thought regarding her slaves, she had momentarily given them credit for the way that they had dressed and presented themselves and in fact was slightly bemused and amazed at how much attention they gave their wardrobe.

The way one looked, the way they wore their hair, and even the way they smelled were all of paramount importance in the arena of courtship. The labor that the enslaved were expected to do was dirty work: toiling in the field all day under the scorching sun of the southern skies; cooking in the big house with the constant heat of the oven and the aroma of the differing foods seeping into clothes, hands, and skin; taking the slops to the pigs with the smell of manure attacking the nostrils and the worn-out shoes provided by the slaveholder proving useless. It was no wonder therefore that slaves, in the context of their working day, soon had clothes that *were all dirt and rags*. However, in the social spaces of courtship, they occupied an alternative identity, one within which they could show off clothes that dazzled, wear ribbons in their hair to beautify themselves, and scatter sweet basil in their clothes to seduce their admirers.

The formerly enslaved Millie Evans related in her WPA interview how the enslaved were able to gain "good-smelling clothes" during slavery times. She recalled that "the way we got our perfume we took rose leaves, Cape jasmines, and sweet basil and laid 'em with our clothes and let 'em stay three or four days, then we had good-smelling clothes that would last too."[45] Similar means were used by the enslaved across the South. Gus Feaster, who was enslaved in South Carolina, told his interviewer that this was one of the ways that the women used to attract the men: "Den de girls charmed us wid honeysuckles and rose petals hid in dere bosoms."

With the intense rivalry surrounding courtship within enslaved communities it was imperative that single men and women look their best on occasions such as dances, frolics, and events where they would socialize with members of the opposite sex. Across the South, enslaved men and women embraced the opportunity to dress up, wear different clothes, adorn themselves with beads and jewelry, and pretty their hair so that they might present a different picture of themselves than the image they were forced to project in the context of their working lives. Gus Feaster recalled that "[i]n dem days dey dried cheneyberries and painted dem and wo' dem on a string around dere necks to charm us."[46] Pick Gladdeny, who was enslaved in Fairfield, South Carolina, recalled that he used to steal away from the plantation to visit a neighboring one where they would be holding a dance. He would be dressed in his best attire; he said he "put on my clean clothes dat was made right on the plantation." He recalled his colorful clothes: "My britches were copprus colored and I had on a home wove

shirt with a pleated bosom. It was dyed red and had wristbands." He also recalled that the girls at the dance would be wearing their homespun stockings and
"dresses so long dat they kivered their shoes."[47] Rhodus Walton, formerly enslaved in Georgia, noted that clothing played an integral part in communicating
one's interest: "Young men always 'cocked' their hats on one side of their heads
when they became interested in the other sex."[48]

Although these events were vital for those among the enslaved who were not
already courting, there were those who had had their intended picked out from
a very young age. Barbara Haywood, who was discussed in the previous chapter, met Frank, her husband, as a young girl when her slaveholder, John Walton, had held a corn shucking. This was where she had first seen Frank. "I wus
a little girl cryin' an' bawlin' an' Frank, who wus a big boy said dat he neber
wanted ter spank a yougin' so bad, an' I ain't liked him no better dan he did
me." Despite this rather disastrous first meeting, their relationship strengthened and intensified throughout their enslavement as they grew up together
and shared their experiences—their laughter and their heartache. After the Civil
War Barbara's family moved to Raleigh, where Frank began working at the city
market. Her meanderings on the way to and from school to see Frank were explained away quite simply by Barbara: "You see I has been in love with him for
a long den."[49]

Barbara's feelings for Frank had been established and consequently flourished during their enslavement. In the aftermath of freedom and when Barbara
had reached a respectable age at which to court, Frank initiated their relationship. Likewise, Lily Perry, who was also discussed in the previous chapter, related
to her interviewer that she and Robert had been raised up together, and she declared, "I loved him frum de time I wus borned."[50] Neither Lily's nor Barbara's
relationship were casual or short-term affairs. They had planted the seed of their
relationship during slavery and watched it grow, no doubt fearing the threat
of sale and separation but nevertheless nurturing the hope that this friendship
might one day flourish into romance and love.

In memory and in practice, the enslaved celebrated their courtships and romances as something which kept them alive. In the literal death that slavery was,
these relationships provided something in the way of joy and excitement, as well
as nervousness and heartache. Not because of the slave system which threatened
sale and separation but in spite of it. The enslaved lived these relationships in the
context of their daily lives as men and women, as individuals, as a people.

Conclusion

Love is or it ain't. Thin love ain't love at all.
Toni Morrison, *Beloved*, 1987

Ah was born back due in slavery so it wasn't for me to fulfil my dreams of what a woman oughta be and to do. Dat's one of de hold-backs of slavery. But nothing can't stop you from wishin'. You can't beat nobody down so low till you can rob 'em of they will.
Zora Neale Hurston, *Their Eyes Were Watching God*, 1937

THE STORIES TOLD within the pages of this book are not fiction—Willis and Mirana Haywood, Mary Bell's parents, Lily and Robert Perry, Barbara and Frank Haywood, Annie Tate's grandparents, Wesley and Minerva Jane, Lucy Ann and Jim Dunn, Tempie and Exter Durham, Lissa and Cleve Lawson were real people. Their stories are true-life narratives reflecting the realities of lives lived under slavery by a people who would have held painful and traumatic memories of their experiences. Stored away in deep chambers of their souls, these memories would only have been recalled with careful and cautious coaxing. These memories were often too painful to bear, but too real to let go. They would have asked themselves and each other, "How long?" Their words would have been only spoken in whispers at first, moving like thieves in the night, stealthy, secretive, cautious. Soon their collective words crafted a history of enslavement which could not speak of the full horrors of what they had endured but which signaled to others that they had survived. They had continued to live.

Within this collective history, however, there were treasured memories—of laughter, of hopefulness, of rejoicing, of love. Strong and durable in reflection, these memories provided balance for the mournful and desperately tragic recollections that ran alongside. These bright memories concerned relationships that had been crafted and cared for from within the very depths of despair. These remembrances celebrated who these people were as individuals, giving meaning to their lives in the fact of retelling, reremembering, reliving. Across the southern states, these two threads were woven into one. The painful wounds reopened, forced to heal under the loving care of those who knew and understood because they too had lived that history. But what of those that had been children born after the question of "how long?" became a triumphant and exulted chorus of "now we are free." How could they ever understand and, indeed, did they even want them to? The other strand of thread served this purpose. This second strand contained the joyful memories of precious and strong relationships, refusing to crack under the extreme pressures that this life had forced upon them. It offered sanctity and salvation to those living this history, seeking refuge from the pain and misery. It contained stories of hope and faith to those children born afterward.

Woven together, these individual strands from across the South created a patchwork quilt of memories. Some of these were too awful to bear, but surrounding them were strands of thread of the most brilliant colors, woven into the most simple and striking designs. This collective memory of enslavement was in turn woven into the fabric of the lives of the formerly enslaved, their children, and their children after that. It was important not to forget the injustices done to them as a people; equally, and perhaps more important, however, it was vital to remember who they were as a people, as a community, as families, as couples, as friends, and as individuals.

Within the collective memories of enslavement, individuals recalled their relationships which had given them strength, protection, nurturance, and love. These were relationships that had been shaped in spite of the pressures of the slave system. The southern institution of slavery had sought to deny humanity to the enslaved men and women across the slaveholding states. It had projected stereotypical images of these men and women that were in fact reliant upon the ways in which slaveholders exploited them but were used to shore up arguments that justified the institution. It had also driven enslaved men and women to utter despair as they had seen countless members of their own families sold away from them because of the slaveholder's pursuit of profit—lovers, husbands, wives, children, near and fictive kin, close friends, and acquaintances. The system of slavery laid bare the pecuniary interests of wealthy white men and women and broke the hearts of many within enslaved communities throughout the South.

And yet, the enslaved continued to live not just existing but building bonds—friendships, romances, kinships, growing together. And everyday they were tortured by unspoken questions of why and how they got to be in this place. Making what they could out of the most impossible circumstances, they built their ties upon landscapes of contested and complex terrains. At times, and with eyes wide open, they would speak of the grief of romance denied and the heartache of lovers parted. However, the collective memories of these relationships also spoke of formidable courage, great hope, and sheer tenacity.

Within their remembrances, the formerly enslaved recalled love as something which had sustained them through the very best and the very worst of times. Love provided them with strength when the will to continue was lost. Faith in the endurance of love supported them when they were feeling hopeless and helpless. Love is hard to define. Its ephemeral and intangible nature, its emotional depths, means that nobody could possibly know or understand how love really feels for the individual. For couples in all places and spaces, the meaning and significance of intimate and private moments are shaped by the contours of both their lives. Thus it was so for the enslaved. This was a history in which they could both share, even if it was for only the briefest of moments in a lifetime. "I wuz married onct 'fore de war by de broom stick ceremony . . . but shucks dey sold away my wife 'fore we'd been married a year."[1] The formerly enslaved Laura Bell claimed in the 1930s that "[l]ove ain't what it uster be by a long shot. . . . 'Cause dar ain't many folks what love all de time."[2] Her parents, Wesley and Minerva Jane, had lived through slavery. They had witnessed the trials that the other one was forced to endure under the crack of the overseer's whip and the authority of "Marse Mack Strickland," who owned the plantation in Mount Airy, Ashe County, where this young couple was enslaved. Laura Bell had located love and its capacity to endure at the center of her narrative. Countless other recollections and remembrances did the same. Alonzo Haywood had done this when he had expressed his incredulity at the fact that some people laughed at the very idea of enslaved couples loving one another. "They should envy the love which kept mother and father so close together in life and even held them in death."[3]

Lucy Ann Dunn, in looking back to her life with Jim, her husband, declared, "I loved him durin' life an' I love now, do he's been daid now for twelve years." Speaking in a voice barely audible to her interviewer, Lucy Ann spoke volumes about the strength and sincerity of her love for Jim: "I can't be here so much any longer now case I'se gittin' too old an' feeble an' I wants ter go ter Jim anyhow. I thinks of him all de time, but seems like we're young agin when I smell honeysuckles or see a yaller moon."[4] These vernacular histories looked backward, recalling the love that had maintained them throughout their lives. They also looked forward, reflecting upon the fact that without the guiding hand of their cherished soulmates it was often difficult to continue with living.

This love shared between these couples—Willis and Mirana Haywood, Mary Bell's parents, Lily and Robert Perry, Barbara and Frank Haywood, Annie Tate's grandparents, Wesley and Minerva Jane, Lucy Ann and Jim Dunn, Tempie and Exter Durham, Lissa and Cleve Lawson—was thick love. Within the concrete realities of enslaved life, they strove to maintain their relationships despite the pressures of that existence. "Love is that condition in the human spirit so profound that it allows me to survive, and better than that, to thrive with passion, compassion, and style,"[5] wrote Maya Angelou. And so it was for the enslaved. They continued to love, and it was the passion, tenderness, and the various ways in which the enslaved communicated this love, that allowed their relationships to flourish. These were the tales that were told across the South, recollected around fireplaces, in kitchens, during family gatherings. Together they formed a collective history of enslavement. Not intended to mask the darker side of what could be remembered, recalled, relived, but rather meant to confirm and affirm the fact that they had survived. They had continued to live. And moreover, and despite their enslavement, they had loved and they had been loved. Enslaved couples found in this love for one another not only the will to survive but also an over-riding reason for their very existence.

Notes

Abbreviations

SHC   Southern Historical Collection, Wilson Library, University of North Carolina, Chapel Hill, N.C.

SFC   Southern Folklore Collection, Wilson Library, University of North Carolina, Chapel Hill, N.C.

SCL   Special Collections Library, Perkins Library, Duke University, Durham, N.C.

Introduction

1. Rawick, *American Slave*, 14 (1): 384.

2. I employ the term "enslaved" in favor of that of "slave" because this research seeks to recognize the personhood of the enslaved man and woman. It has been argued that the term slave has "facilitated the fashioning of a limited discourse of victimhood . . . that has relied on unjust stereotypical notions of biological, geographical and linguistic notions of African 'inferiority.'" See Campbell, "Voicing Slavery: Writing the Caribbean and Its Diaspora in the New Millennium." Alternatively the term "enslaved" is suggestive of the power relations inherent in the system of slavery and also recognizes the capabilities of the individuals concerned. I do, however, deploy the term "slave" on occasion, in particular when discussing slaveholders' perceptions of their human chattel. It would be anachronistic to impose a modern interpretation of the term slave onto slaveholders' evaluation of their labor force. Indeed, the majority of slaveholders did perceive their work force as slaves rather than as enslaved individuals possessed of full or partial agency, and therefore defined them within stereotypes based on notions of inferiority. Also see Camp, *Closer to Freedom*, Introduction, fn. 2.

3. Rawick, *American Slave*, 14 (1): 384.

4. Ellen Rothman has provided a working definition for the concept of courtship in which she distinguishes between *courting* behavior and the *courtship* relationship. Rothman defines courting behavior as those relationships of a more "casual or communal nature." She contrasts this to *courtship*, which she uses to refer to "activities that were *expected* to lead to marriage." See Rothman, "Sex and Self-Control," 410 (emphasis in original). I have not attended to such nuances when employing such terms and have used both "courting" and "courtship" to refer to those relationships between mutually consenting enslaved men and women that were grounded in feelings of intimacy and affection. Certainly, there were levels of expectation from the enslaved community, family members, and masters and mistresses, regarding the idea that certain relationships would lead to something more formalized, while other affairs were perhaps perceived as more casual in nature. However, several other factors, such as the slaves' legal status in the South, which defined them as property and hence unable to legally form contracts such as marriage, and the influence of the slaveholder over the ways in which enslaved couples might have informally validated their union, inevitably impacted on the ways in which the enslaved defined and managed their courtships. It would therefore prove problematic to assess the differences between *courting* behavior and *courtships* for the enslaved.

5. See Scott, *Weapons of the Weak* and *Domination and the Arts of Resistance*. For a brilliant discussion of the uses of everyday resistance by enslaved women see Camp, *Closer to Freedom*.

6. Since the 1970s there has been an immense amount of work focusing upon the enslaved family. Discussions have mainly focused around the enslaved family unit as a separate and viable institution and whether there were regional differences or external factors that affected the ability of the enslaved to maintain these familial bonds, see Labinjoh, "The Sexual Life of the Oppressed: An Examination of the Family Life of Ante-Bellum Slaves"; Genovese, *Roll Jordan Roll: The World the Slaves Made*; Gutman, *The Black Family in Slavery and Freedom*; Brown, "Sexuality and the Slave Community"; Burton, *In My Father's House Are Many Mansions*; Durrill, "Slavery, Kinship, and Dominance."; Malone, *Sweet Chariot: Slave Family and Household Structure in Nineteenth-Century Louisiana*; Dusinberre, *Them Dark Days*; Hudson, *To Have and To Hold*; Patterson, *Rituals of Blood*, chapter 1, "Broken Bloodlines"; Ball, *Slaves in the Family*; Dunaway, *The African-American Family in Slavery and Freedom*; West, *Chains of Love*.

7. Stowe, *Intimacy and Power*, 50.

8. For further discussion of the ways in which slaveholders sought to control the reproductive capacities of enslaved women, see Schwartz, *Birthing a Slave*, esp. chapter 1, "Procreation."

9. See for example, Stone, *The Family, Sex, and Marriage*; Degler, *At Odds*, esp. chapter 1, "The Emergence of the Modern American Family"; Fliegelman, *Prodigals and Pilgrims*, chapter 5, "Affectionate Unions and the New Voluntarism"; Lewis, *The Pursuit of Happiness*, chapter 5, "Earthly Connexions—Love"; Rothman, *Hands and Hearts*; Censer, *North Carolina Planters*, chapter 5, "Courtship and Marriage among the Planters' Offspring; Mintz and Kellogg, *Domestic Revolutions*. The focus of debate for historians of the antebellum southern white family is whether the hierarchical structure, which ordained that white women, children, and slaves were subservient to white male authority, prevented romantic love or affection from becoming the major determinants in southern emotional experiences. Some historians have diluted the image of a "ruling patriarch," using instead the idea of paternalism to define the character of relationships within the southern household. For an example of this argument see Genovese, *The World the Slaveholders Made* and *Roll Jordan Roll*; also see Fox-Genovese, *Within the Plantation Household*. Other historians have argued that the southern planter family diverged little from that of its northern counterparts. Love and affection were cast as the ideal, if not the only, legitimate basis for marriage or establishing a relationship. For an example of this argument see, Censer, *North Carolina Planters*, chapter 4, "Courtship and Marriage among the Planters' Offspring." A separate line of historical enquiry has concentrated upon the white planter class within their distinct social world rather than attempting to position them within an analysis of wider North American society. See, Stowe, "The Rhetoric of Authority" and *Intimacy and Power*, esp. chapter 2, "Courtship, Sexuality, and Feeling." Stowe argued that the white southern elite may have shared the values current in the northern states during the first half of the nineteenth century, such as the increasing importance of the family and the ideal of the companionate marriage, yet these values were differently shaped and understood in the South, because of the system of slavery, which necessitated the expression of power and authority in every action, word, and thought.

10. Jacobs, *Incidents in the Life of a Slave Girl*, 58, 59, 65–66.

11. "The Experience of Rev. Thomas H. Jones Who Was a Slave for Forty-Three Years," 229.

12. Rawick, *American Slave*, 1, "From Sundown to Sunup," 70.

13. Rawick, *American Slave*, 15 (2): 32.

14. Ibid. 78.

15. "Born in Slavery: Slave Narratives from the Federal Writers' Project," South Carolina Narratives, 14 (4), 243, http://memory.loc.gov/ammem/snhtml/snhome.html.

16. Rawick, *American Slave*, 14 (1): 360.

17. "Born in Slavery: Slave Narratives from the Federal Writers' Project," Missouri Narratives, 10, 25, http://memory.loc.gov/ammem/snhtml/snhome.html.

18. Rawick, *American Slave*, 15 (2): 333–34.

19. I apply the term "enslaved household" as encompassing not just a physical structure or a composition of individuals related through familial ties, but also the sense of community which was cultivated among groups of enslaved men and women who lived in close proximity to one another and the different landscapes upon which enslaved men and women actively courted one another within this community. See Battle, "A Yard to Sweep," 102–3.

20. Penningroth, "My People, My People"; also see Penningroth, *The Claims of Kinfolk*.

21. "Born in Slavery: Slave Narratives from the Federal Writers' Project," South Carolina Narratives, 14 (1), 231, http://memory.loc.gov/ammem/snhtml/snhome.html.

22. White, *Ar'n't I a Woman?*, 154.

23. Hudson, *To Have and to Hold*, 144.

24. Ibid. 158.

25. "Born in Slavery: Slave Narratives from the Federal Writers' Project," South Carolina Narratives, 14 (3), 49, http://memory.loc.gov/ammem/snhtml/snhome.html.

26. Olmstead, *A Journey to the Seaboard Slave States*, 367.

27. Camp, *Closer to Freedom*, 8.

28. Census of North Carolina, 1830, Christian Almanac for North Carolina, 1832, 17–18, SCL.

29. Taylor, *Slaveholding in North Carolina*, 35–36.

30. Johnson, *Ante-bellum North Carolina*, 53.

31. Durrill, "Routine of Seasons: Labor Regimes and Social Ritual in an Antebellum Plantation Community," 165.

32. Cited in Johnson, *Ante-bellum North Carolina*, 21.

33. Sarah F. Hicks Williams, to Mr. & Mrs. Samuel Hicks, 17 November 1853, Sarah F. Hicks Williams Letters, fol. 4, 1853, SHC.

34. See Johnson, *Ante-Bellum North Carolina*, 55, 468.

35. For further discussion on the nature and significance of cross-plantation unions for the enslaved in South Carolina see West, *Chains of Love*, chapter 5, "Enforced Separations"

36. Cary and Kay, *Slavery in North Carolina*, 161.

37. Stearns and Lewis, *An Emotional History*, 12.

38. Faulkner, *Absalom, Absalom!*, 100–101.

39. Ibid. 101.

40. Hudson, *To Have and to Hold*, 166.

41. Edward E. Baptist, "Stol' and Fetched Here," 245.

42. Yetman, "The Background of the Slave Narrative Collection," 534.

43. B. A. Botkin, [ed.], *Lay My Burden Down*, 59.

44. Spindel, "Assessing Memory: Twentieth-Century Slave Narratives Reconsidered," 252.

45. Escott, *Slavery Remembered*, 6. Also. see Escott, "The Art and Science of Reading WPA Slave Narratives."

46. Botkin, *Lay My Burden Down*, 59.

47. Baptist, "Stol' and Fetched Here," 245.

48. Escott, *Slavery Remembered*, 7.

49. Blassingame, *The Slave Community*.

50. Blassingame, "Using the Testimony of Ex-Slaves: Approaches and Problems," 482.

51. Musher, "Contesting 'The Way the Almighty Wants It,'" quote taken from 2.
52. Baptist, "Stol' and Fetched Here," 247.
53. Blassingame, "Using the Testimony of Ex-Slaves," 487–88.
54. Ibid. 489. Also see Escott, *Slavery Remembered*; Musher, "Contesting 'The Way the Almighty Wants It'"
55. Ibid. 488.
56. Rawick, *American Slave*, 11: xli.
57. David Bailey, "A Divided Prism: Two Sources of Black Testimony on Slavery." Bailey compared a selection of the WPA collection with a sample of longer slave narratives. He argued that the longer slave narratives more accurately depicted the system of slavery because they represent "middle aged recollections of the recent past." Bailey further argued that the WPA collection provided a picture of a more complacent and submissive slave society than do the longer autobiographies. He suggested that there was a lack of emphasis on slave resistance in the WPA collection in comparison to the longer narratives, which documented several instances of overt and active resistance such as running away. However, we must question Bailey's interpretation of the WPA collection and his definition of "resistance." The WPA collections did detail numerous episodes of "resistance" such as evading the patrollers, leaving the plantation without a pass, and meeting at secret gatherings in the slave quarters. Although these acts did not impact on the system of slavery in the same manner as running away, they must still be considered in terms of acts of daily resistance intended to ameliorate the conditions of enslavement.
58. Woodward, "History from Slave Sources," 473.
59. Rawick, *American Slave*, 11: xxviii.
60. Baptist, "Stol' and Fetched Here," 247.
61. Ibid. 245.
62. Ibid. 263.
63. See Hadden, *Slave Patrols*.

Chapter 1. "Love Seems with Them More to Be an Eager Desire": Racialized Stereotypes in the Slaveholding South

1. Morgan, "Some Could Suckle," 168. The same essay also appears in an edited collection of essays by Stephanie M. H. Camp and Edward E. Baptist, *New Studies in the History of American Slavery*. Also see Morgan, *Laboring Women: Gender and Reproduction in New World Slavery*, chapter 1.
2. Ibid. 167.
3. Ligon, *A True and Exact History*, 51.
4. John Mandeville, cited in Morgan, "Some Could Suckle," 170.
5. Jordan, *White Over Black*, 150.
6. "Jamaica, a Poem, in Three Parts . . . ," (London, 1777), cited in ibid.
7. For a further discussion of the image of the "black Jezebel" and the gendered stereotypes that the elite slaveholding classes held of their slaves see White, *Ar'n't I a Woman?*, esp. chapter 1, "Jezebel and Mammy: The Mythology of Female Slavery"; Fox-Genovese, *Within the Plantation Household*, 290–302. Clinton, "Southern Dishonour."
8. For further discussion see, Brown, *Good Wives, Nasty Wenches, and Anxious Patriarchs*, esp. chapter 4, "Engendering Racial Difference" and chapter 6, "From 'Foul Crimes' to 'Spurious Issues': Sexual Regulation and the Social Construction of Race."
9. Welter, "The Cult of True Womanhood," 313, 315.
10. See Jordan, *White Over Black*, chapter 4, "Fruits of Passion"; Clinton, "Southern Dishonour."

11. Jacobs, *Incidents in the Life*, 26, 28. For a comprehensive and insightful examination of the life of Harriet Jacobs see Yellin, *Harriet Jacobs, A Life*.

12. Fox-Genovese, *Within the Plantation Household*, 292.

13. White, *Ar'n't I a Woman?*, 176.

14. T. J. Macon, *Life Gleanings*, 6, electronic edition. This work is the property of the University of North Carolina at Chapel Hill. It may be used freely by individuals for research, teaching, and personal use as long as this statement of availability is included in the text, http://docsouth.unc.edu/macon/macon.html.

15. Thomas Nelson Page, *Social Life in Old Virginia before the War*, 59–60, electronic edition. This work is the property of the University of North Carolina at Chapel Hill. It may be used freely by individuals for research, teaching, and personal use as long as this statement of availability is included in the text, http://docsouth.unc.edu/southlit/pagesocial/page.html.

16. Rebecca Latimer Felton, *Country Life in Georgia in the Days of My Youth*, 98, electronic edition. This work is the property of the University of North Carolina at Chapel Hill. It may be used freely by individuals for research, teaching, and personal use as long as this statement of availability is included in the text, http://docsouth.unc.edu/fpn/felton/felton.html (emphasis added).

17. White, *Ar'n't I a Woman?*, 61.

18. Beckles, "Centering Woman: The Political Economy of Gender in West African and Caribbean Slavery," 97.

19. Ibid. 95.

20. For a further discussion of the ways in which West African gender norms were disrupted by the work regimes imposed on the enslaved in the American South and possible enslaved resistance and reaction to this, see Pearson, "A Countryside Full of Flames."

21. Important exceptions to this were yeoman women who frequently worked in the fields performing agricultural labor, either alongside other members of her family and/or a small number of slaves. Stephanie McCurry, *Masters of Small Worlds*, argues that in the context of antebellum South Carolina, the work yeoman women performed in the fields represented a transgression against white womanhood, and thus was "customarily ignored and even denied. A collusive silence surrounded one of the labor practices that most clearly distinguished yeoman farms from plantations, that set yeoman wives and daughters apart from their planter counterparts, that dangerously eroded the social distinctions between free women and slaves, and that cut deeply into the pride of men raised in a culture of honor"(81). Within antebellum North Carolina these distinctions would have been less pronounced, with smaller plantations and farms dominating the landscape, and only a limited number of slaveholders owning over fifty slaves (576 in 1850) primarily in counties such as Wake, Washington, and Halifax; see U.S. Census Office, "Agriculture in the US in 1860," 235–36, cited in Johnson, *Ante-Bellum North Carolina*, 55. Thus, white women would have worked alongside their families and their slaves on their land more frequently than those in South Carolina. However, the ideal of the southern lady was maintained throughout the antebellum period across the entire South and was held up as the epitome of white womanhood, to which all women should aspire to. Thus, the "collusive silence" surrounding yeoman women's work in the fields of South Carolina would to a certain extent also have been maintained in North Carolina.

22. Rawick, *American Slave*, 14 (1): 92–93.

23. Ibid. 15 (2): 31.

24. Ibid. 14, (1): 394.

25. For a discussion of the sexual division of labor and the gendered nature of work among the enslaved see Jones, *Labor of Love, Labor of Sorrow*, chapter 1, "My Mother Was Much of a Woman: Slavery"; White, *Ar'n't I a Woman?*, chapter 2, "The Nature of Female Slavery,"

and chapter 3, "The Life Cycle of the Female Slave"; Perrin, "Slave Women and Work in the American South."

26. This is one of the fundamental points that Gutman made in his arguments concerning the slave family in the antebellum South. He stated that, "slave belief and behavior at the emancipation were the consequence of a recurrent action between accumulating historical experiences (culture) as transmitted over time through an adaptive slave-family and kinship system and the changing slave society in which the slaves lived." see Gutman, *The Black Family in Slavery and Freedom*, 34.

27. Brown, *Good Wives, Nasty Wenches, and Anxious Patriarchs*, 132–35.

28. Burnham, "An Impossible Marriage," 205.

29. See White, *Ar'n't I a Woman?*, 142–46.

30. Jacobs, *Incidents in the Life*, 11 (emphasis in original).

31. Cited in White, *Ar'n't I a Woman?*, 146.

32. Blassingame, *The Slave Community*, chapter 5, "Plantation Stereotypes and Institutional Roles."

33. Henry K. Burgwyn Jr to Anna Burgwyn, 3 April 1859, Burgwyn Family Papers, 1787– 1987, fol. 4, 1858–1859, SHC (emphasis in original). The "Ganemede" that Henry Burgywn refers to is probably that of "Ganymede," a young Trojan in Greek mythology, whom the Gods made immortal and was taken up to heaven as their cupbearer. The term as it is implied in this quotation is heavily loaded with sarcasm.

34. For a discussion of the competing images of black masculinity in the American South see Blassingame, *The Slave Community*, chapter 5, "Plantation Stereotypes and Institutional Roles," chapter 6, "Plantation Realities," and chapter 7, "Slave Personality Types." For a dated discussion of the image of Sambo see, Elkins, *Slavery, A Problem in American Institutional and Intellectual Life*, 82.

35. Francis Cope Yarnell, "Letters on Slavery," (1853), Francis Cope Yarnell Papers, SCL.

36. See Fox-Genovese, *Within the Plantation Household*, 291; also see Jordan, *White Over Black*, 151–64.

37. Anna Bingham to Mary (Bingham) Lynch, 8 February 1839, Thomas and Mary Bingham Lynch Papers, box 1, fol.3, correspondence 1838–1843, SCL.

38. See Hodes, *White Women, Black Men*; Sommerville, "The Rape Myth in the Old South Reconsidered." She also expanded upon these arguments and illustrated the more complex and nuanced relationships between southern whites and the enslaved in her recently published monograph, *Rape and Race in the Nineteenth-Century South*. Also see Bardaglio, "Rape and the Law in the Old South" and "Shamefull Matches."

39. Sommerville, "The Rape Myth," 485.

40. Thomas Jefferson, "Notes on the State of Virginia," 98.

41. Gary Wills, "Did Tocqueville 'Get' America?" 53. Gary Wills suggests that Tocqueville's visit to the southern states was extremely brief, initially turning South in December 1830, to find his access blocked by severe freezing of the rivers and snowdrifts. Tocqueville spent only one day each in Cincinnati, Louisville, Nashville, Memphis, and Mobile, and his longest stay was just four days in Washington D.C. Nevertheless, as Wills perceptively argues, "Fleeting as was this exposure to the South, it was sufficient for Tocqueville to pick up all the prejudices of the region" (53).

Chapter 2. Asking Master Mack to Court: Competing Spheres of Influence

1. Sarah E. Devereux to Thomas Devereux, 4 December 1840, Devereux Family Papers, fol. 3, correspondence 1791–1841, SCL.

2. Rawick, *American Slave*, 15 (2): 9.

3. "Narrative of the Life of Moses Grandy," 162.

4. John White, interviewed at Sand Springs, Oklahoma, cited in Yetman, *Voices from Slavery*, 306.

5. "Born in Slavery: Slave Narratives from the Federal Writers' Project," Alabama Narratives, 1, 381, http://memory.loc.gov/ammem/snhtml/snhome.html. Mollie Tillman who related these painful memories also recalled the sheer sense of overwhelming joy she had felt when, on moving to Alabama after freedom from the plantation in Georgia which she and her family had been enslaved upon, she met up quite unexpectedly with her former love, "I runned up on him. I wuz so happy I shouted all over dat meeetin' house. We jes' tuck up whar we lef' off an 'fo' long us got married." (382). Unfortunately this was not the experience of many among the enslaved and they were very often forced to face the reality that they would never see these people ever again.

6. Sarah F. Hicks Williams to Mr. and Mrs. Samuel Hicks, 22 May 1855, Sarah F. Hicks Williams Letters, fol. 5, 1854–1855, SHC.

7. Rawick, *American Slave*, 14 (1): 77.

8. Gutman, *The Black Family*, especially chapter 1, "Send Me Some of the Children's Hair"; Tadman, *Speculators and Slaves*, 174.

9. Breeden, *Advice among Masters*, 239.

10. Southron, "The Policy of the Southern Planter," cited in Breeden, *Advice among Masters*, 243.

11. Camp, *Closer to Freedom*, chapter 1, "A Geography of Containment: The Bondage of Space and Time."

12. Southron, "The Policy of the Southern Planter," cited in Breeden, *Advice among Masters*, 243

13. Anon., "On the Management of Slaves," cited in ibid. 240.

14. A Mississippi Planter, "Management of Negroes upon Southern Estate," 10, *De Bow's Review*, (June 1851), 621–27, 626, University of Michigan: Making of America Project, http://name.umdl.umich.edu/acg1336.1-10.006.

15. St. George Cocke, "Plantation Management—Police," 14, *De Bow's Review*, (February 1853), 177–78, 178, University of Michigan: Making of America Project, http://name.umdl.umich.edu/acg1336.1-14.002.

16. "Rules of the Plantation," cited in Breeden, *Advice among Masters*, 248.

17. See Smith, *Mastered by the Clock*.

18. For a brilliant, insightful, and lively analysis concerning the ways in which "sounds" were remembered by the formerly enslaved during slavery see White and White, *The Sounds of Slavery*.

19. Rawick, *American Slave*, 15 (2): 35.

20. Ibid. 144.

21. Smith, *Mastered by the Clock*, 123.

22. Rawick, *American Slave*, 15 (2): 188.

23. Ibid. 14 (1): 101.

24. Allen Parker, *Recollections of Slavery Times*, 22–27, electronic edition. This work is the property of the University of North Carolina at Chapel Hill. It may be used freely by individuals for research, teaching, and personal use as long as this statement of availability is included in the text, http://docsouth.unc.edu/neh/parker/parker.html.

25. "Born in Slavery: Slave Narratives from the Federal Writers' Project," South Carolina Narratives, 14 (4): 53, http://memory.loc.gov/ammem/snhtml/snhome.html.

26. Robert Collins, "Essay on the Treatment and Management of Slaves," cited in Breeden, *Advice among Masters*, 23.

27. Ethelred Philips to James Philips, 21 December 1863, James Jones Philips Papers, series 1, fol. 2, SHC.

28. "Born in Slavery: Slave Narratives from the Federal Writers' Project," Georgia Narratives, 4 (1), 175, http://memory.loc.gov/ammem/snhtml/snhome.html.

29. Rawick, *American Slave*, 15 (2): 171.

30. "Narrative of the Life and Adventures of Henry Bibb," 456–57.

31. Rawick, *American Slave*, 1, (SS): 30.

32. Anna Bingham to Mary (Bingham) Lynch, 30 March 1832, Thomas and Mary Bingham Lynch Papers, box 1, fol. 2, correspondence 1830–1837, SCL.

33. 12 May 1832, ibid.

34. "Aunt Sally or Cross the Way of Freedom," 50–51.

35. See Censer, *North Carolina Planters*, chapter 4, "Courtship and Marriage among the Planters' Offspring."

36. Laura Norwood to Col. Thomas and Louisa Lenoir, 11 February 1840, Lenoir Family Papers, series 1.2, box 6, fol. 78, January–March 1840, SHC. Laura Norwood's use of the phrase, "wearing the willow" refers to Elia being abandoned by his lover, Eliza. The term derives from a belief that lovers forsaken by or having lost their beloved wore a wreath of willow to demonstrate their grief—"And I must wear the willow garland for him that's dead or false to me," Thomas Campbell, "Adelgitha," (c. 1777–1844), sourced from website Oldpoetry.com, http://oldpoetry.com/authors/Thomas%20Campbell.

37. Laura Norwood to Louisa Lenoir, November 1840, ibid., series 1.2, box 6, fol. 80, October–December 1840.

38. For the purpose of this research I shall limit my definition of religion to the Protestant faith, namely Methodist, Baptist, and Presbyterian. Protestantism has been commonly defined as the dominant religion in the Old South among both white and black southerners, however there are certain scholars who would disagree with this argument. For further reading see, Frazier, *Negro Church*; Matthews, "The Methodist Mission" and *Religion in the Old South*; Raboteau, *Slave Religion* and "Slave Autonomy and Religion"; Sobel, *Trabelin' on: The Slave Journey*; Joyner, *Down by the River Side*; Bailey, "Protestantism and Afro-Americans in the Old South"; Little, "George Liele and the Rise of Independent Black Baptist Churches"; Johnson, "A Delusive Clothing"; Frey and Wood, *Come Shouting to Zion*.

39. Cited in Nickens, "The Slave Religious Experience," 46.

40. Charles Colcock Jones, Thirteenth Annual Report of the Association for the Religious Instruction of the Negroes in Liberty Co. Georgia, 1848, SCL. Quotes taken from 13–23 (emphasis in original). Although this report focused upon the slave communities of Liberty County, Georgia, it was intended to reach a much larger audience and would have been used widely in the South as religious dogma relating to the entire slave populations who were members of the Presbyterian Church.

41. Ibid. 18–19.

42. Ibid. 19, 23 (emphasis in original).

43. Smith, "Church Organization as an Agency of Social Control," 101.

44. Sawyers Creek Baptist Church Records, Camden County, Vol. 1, 31 July 1815–13 November 1853, SHC.

45. Minutes from meetings of April and May 1848, Wheelers (Wheeleys) Baptist Church Minute Book, Vol. 2, SHC.

46. Smith, "Church Organization as an Agency of Social Control," 311, 305.

47. See ibid. 304–41.

48. Ibid. 312.

49. Sawyers Creek Baptist Church Records, Camden County, Vol. 1, 31 July 1815–13 November 1853, SHC.

50. Ibid., 8 February 1845, 9 September 1858.

51. Rawick, *American Slave*, 15 (2): 3.

52. Ibid. 360.

53. There has been a limited amount of work produced upon the power of gossip and rumor in the context of the United States. This work has focused most notably on the colonial context within the white communities of the eastern seaboard, see Stoler, "In Cold Blood." For an excellent discussion of the ways in which hearsay and supposed scandals could operate at the local markets in National Georgia, particularly among enslaved women "hucksters:" selling their wares see, Wood, *Gender, Race, and Rank in a Revolutionary Age.*

54. Hudson, *To Have and to Hold,* 140.

55. Parker, *Recollections of Slavery Times,* electronic addition, 23. This work is the property of the University of North Carolina at Chapel Hill. It may be used freely by individuals for research, teaching, and personal use as long as this statement of availability is included in the text, http://docsouth.unc.edu/neh/parker/parker.html.

56. "Born in Slavery: Slave Narratives from the Federal Writers' Project," South Carolina Narratives, 14 (3), 167, http://memory.loc.gov/ammem/snhtml/snhome.html.

57. "Born in Slavery: Slave Narratives from the Federal Writers' Project," Georgia Narratives, 4 (2), 296, http://memory.loc.gov/ammem/snhtml/snhome.html.

58. Rawick, *American Slave,* 14 (1): 101.

59. Ibid.

60. Ibid. 281.

61. Ibid. 282.

62. Ibid. 191. This particular practice of carrying vessels or goods on one's head, especially for women, may well have derived from West African heritage and thus possibly serves as an example of cultural retention among the enslaved.

63. Yetman, *Voices from Slavery,* 85.

64. "Born in Slavery: Slave Narratives from the Federal Writers' Project," South Carolina Narratives, 14 (1), 243–44, http://memory.loc.gov/ammem/snhtml/snhome.html.

65. Weston, "Management of a Southern Plantation," 44.

66. Walter Waightsill Lenoir to Selina Avery Lenoir, 15 January 1864, Lenoir Family Papers, Personal Correspondence, Box 1.3, fol. 154–55, 1861–1865, SHC.

67. Fett, *Working Cures,* 6, 85

68. Rawick, *American Slave,* 15 (2): 121.

69. Ibid. 361.

70. Sharla Fett notes that the mention of witches and conjuring activities performed by witches was much more frequent in the North Carolina WPA narratives than those from Georgia, South Carolina or Virginia, see *Working Cures,* 85, fn.5. Without further research it is impossible to explain this pattern; however, one might hypothesize that the origins of the enslaved in North Carolina played some part in this. North Carolina's lack of access to the Atlantic meant that it was largely dependent on the neighboring states of South Carolina and Virginia to provide its slaves, rather than importing them directly from Africa. However, North Carolina did import a sizable number of slaves directly from the Caribbean, particularly Jamaica, during the eighteenth century, see Minchinton, "The Seaborne Slave Trade of North Carolina." Consequently, cultural customs, ideals, and practices of the enslaved in North Carolina may have owed much more to the Caribbean Islands than for those enslaved elsewhere in the American South, hence a stronger belief in certain aspects of the supernatural such as witches. This argument is supported by the existence of the John Kooner parades by the enslaved in North Carolina, which have not been documented as occurring anywhere else on the North American mainland. For further discussion see Long, *The History of Jamaica* (1774); Warren, "A Doctor's Experience in Three Continents"; Cameron, "Christmas on an Old Plantation"; Macmillan, "John Kuners"; Dirks, *The Black Saturnalia*; Fenn, "A Perfect Equality Seemed to Reign"; Durrill, "Routine of Seasons."

71. Rawick, *American Slave*, 15 (2): 405.

72. Ibid. 298.

73. "Narrative of the Life and Adventures of Henry Bibb," 450–51.

74. "Born in Slavery: Slave Narratives from the Federal Writers' Project," Georgia Narratives, 4 (4), 266. http://memory.loc.gov/ammem/snhtml/snhome.html.

75. For further discussion concerning the themes of contest and competition within the folklore of the enslaved, see Levine, *Black Culture and Black Consciousness*, chapter 2, "The Meaning of Slave Tales"; Levine, "Some Go Up and Some Go Down"; Griffin, "Courtship Contests and the Meaning of Conflict in the Folklore of Slaves."

76. Fett, *Working Cures*, 12.

Chapter 3. Getting Out to Play and Courting All They Pleased: The Social and Temporal Geographies of Enslaved Courtship

1. Rawick, *American Slave*, 15 (2): 422.

2. See Griffin, "Goin' Back Over There to See That Girl."

3. Cited in Outland, "Slavery, Work, and the Geography of the North Carolina Naval Stores Industry," 27. Outland expands upon his arguments concerning the naval stores industry in North Carolina in his monograph, *Tapping the Pines*, published in 2004.

4. Durrill, "Routine of Seasons," 166.

5. See Hudson, *To Have and To Hold*, chapter 1, "For Better or Worse: Slaves' World of Work."

6. Rawick, *American Slave*, 14 (1): 74–75.

7. Ibid. 121.

8. Jonathan Worth to David Gaston Worth, 25 June 1853, Worth Family Papers, fol. 3, 1853–1856, SCL.

9. Outland, "Slavery, Work, and the Geography of the North Carolina Naval Stores Industry," 43.

10. Rawick, *American Slave*, 15 (2): 15.

11. Ibid. 14 (1): 285.

12. Ibid. 288.

13. Davidson Family Papers, box 3, fol. 1, correspondence, nd, and receipts, 1802–1877, SCL.

14. Cronly Family Papers, box 1, fol. 1, SCL.

15. McRae Plantation Memorandum Book, SCL.

16. Rawick, *American Slave*, 14 (1): 29.

17. Ibid. 9.

18. Jacobs, *Incidents in the Life*, 14.

19. Camp, "Pleasures of Resistance," 534; also see Camp, *Closer to Freedom*, chapter 1, "A Geography of Containment: The Bondage of Space and Time."

20. Cary and Kay, *Slavery in North Carolina*, 63.

21. Hadden, *Slave Patrols*, 34–35.

22. Cited in Cary and Kay, *Slavery in North Carolina*, 69.

23. For further discussion of the patrol gangs in North Carolina, see Hadden, *Slave Patrols*, esp. chapters 2, 3, and 4.

24. Breeden, *Advice among Masters*, 243.

25. Tattler, "Management of Negroes," cited in Ibid. 249.

26. Rawick, *American Slave*, 14 (1): 4.

27. Ibid. 15 (2): 186.

28. Camp, "Pleasures of Resistance," 534.

29. Rawick, *American Slave*, 15 (2): 233.

30. Ibid. 146.

31. Ibid. 310.

32. Walvin, "Slaves, Free Time and the Question of Leisure," 12.

33. Ibid.

34. Rawick, *American Slave*, 15 (2): 365.

35. Ibid. 14 (1): 209 (emphasis added).

36. A Mississippi Planter, "Management of Negroes upon Southern Estate," 10, *De Bow's Review*, (June 1851), 621–27, 625, University of Michigan: Making of America Project, http://name.umdl.umich.edu/acg1336.1-10.006.

37. "Born in Slavery: Slave Narratives from the Federal Writers' Project," Georgia Narratives, 4 (3), 206, http://memory.loc.gov/ammem/snhtml/snhome.html.

38. Rawick, *American Slave*, 15 (2): 31 (emphasis added).

39. Ibid. 14 (1): 28 (emphasis added).

40. Ibid. 15 (2): 366.

41. Ibid. 339.

42. Ibid. 336.

43. Ibid. 14 (1): 83.

44. It has been argued that the Kooner parades originated in Africa, their namesake being John Conny, a tribal headsman on the Guinea Coast around 1720. However, other historians have stressed the European influences in the parade such as the actor boy character. There is also a suggestion that the name John Kooner is a corruption of the term *gens inconnus* (unknown folks) signifying those hidden behind the John Kooner masks. For a further discussion of the John Kooner parades, their origins and meanings see Long, *The History of Jamaica*, vol. 2, 424; Warren, "A Doctor's Experience in Three Continents," 200–203; Macmillan, "John Kuners"; Dirks, *The Black Saturnalia*: Durrill, "Routine of Seasons."

45. See Minchinton, "The Seaborne Slave Trade of North Carolina."

46. Warren, "A Doctor's Experience in Three Continents," 201.

47. Anne Cameron to Paul Cameron, 8 January 1848, Cameron Family Papers, box 44, fol. 1024, 1–15 January 1848, SHC.

48. Rebecca Cameron, "Christmas on an Old Plantation," 5.

49. Fenn, "A Perfect Equality Seemed to Reign."

50. Jacobs, *Incidents in the Life*, 99.

51. Fenn, "A Perfect Equality Seemed to Reign," 137.

52. Henry King Burgwyn to M. Arthur Souter, 6 August 1843, Burgwyn Family Papers, fol. 1, correspondence, 1787, 1843, 1846, SHC.

53. William Pettigrew to Moses and Henry, 18 December 1857, Pettigrew Family Papers, box 10, fol. 207, December 1857, SHC.

54. Cited in Durrill, "Routine of Seasons," 166.

55. Camp, "Pleasures of Resistance," 535; also see Camp, *Closer to Freedom*, chapter 3, "The Intoxication of Pleasurable Amusements: Secret Parties and the Politics of the Body."

56. See Battle, "A Yard to Sweep," quote taken from 130.

57. Of course, it was unlikely that slaveholders were completely unaware of these practices and may even have turned a blind eye to them on occasion. However, it was the enslaved's *desire* for social spaces that they could call their own that is significant. Also the ways in which the enslaved resisted and redefined the slaveholders' authorized spaces in favor of their own.

58. Rawick, *American Slave*, 15 (2): 156.

59. See Davis, *Women, Raced and Class*, 17.

60. Interview with Leon Berry, Long Creek, North Carolina, Glenn Hinson Collection, SFC.

61. Sarah F. Hicks Williams to Mr. And Mrs. Samuel Hicks, 25 March 1859, Sarah F. Hicks Williams Letters, fol. 6, 1856–1868, SHC.

62. Tattler, "Management of Negroes," cited in Breeden, *Advice among Masters*, 76.

63. Rawick, *American Slave*, 15 (2): 402–3.

64. See Frey and Wood, *Come Shouting to Zion*.

65. Perhaps the most famed African American preacher of the slaveholding South was Henry Evans. Evans was a free black, a shoemaker by trade and a zealous Methodist who refused to separate white and black in church. See Parkinson, "The Religious Instruction of Slaves."

66. Aside from references within the narratives of the formerly enslaved pertaining to the overall nature of the invisible institution it was difficult to understand exactly how courtship might have unfolded in this context. I have little doubt that the enslaved took the opportunity to court within these social spaces, especially as it was located within the same social spaces as illicit frolics—the quarters of the enslaved or locations beyond the plantation—but the evidence for such occurrences is difficult to unearth. Thus, I have focused my analysis upon the authorized social spaces of more visible aspects of enslaved religious practice.

67. Battle, [ed.], *Memories of an Old-Time Tar Heel*, 125.

68. Sawyers Creek Baptist Church Records, Camden County, Vol. 1, 31 July 1815–13 November 1853, SHC.

69. Rawick, *American Slave*, 14 (1): 265.

70. See for example, Rawick, *American Slave*, 14 (1): 190; 15 (2): 40; 15 (2): 187.

71. Particularly pertinent to this point is Camp's advocating the use of imagination in the reading of sources derived from the formerly enslaved. She writes that "as we work with our written evidence—whether it remains in shards or in linear feet—we can also employ the imagination, closely reading our documents in their context and speculating about their meanings." See Camp, *Closer to Freedom*, 95.

72. Rawick, *American Slave*, 14 (1): 386.

73. Ibid. 281.

Chapter 4. *Taking a Whipping for Lily: Courtship as a Narrative of Resistance*

1. Rawick, *American Slave*, 15 (2): 163–65.

2. There has been a recent renaissance in the use of the concept of "resistance" in relation to the enslaved. Pioneered by Bauer and Bauer, in their article for the *Journal of Negro History*, "Day to Day Resistance to Slavery" (1942), these ideas were reawakened by the likes of Stanley Engerman in his "Concluding Reflections" in Hudson's *Working Towards Freedom* published in 1994. Engerman considered the question of how far we should consider any autonomous action undertaken by the enslaved as resisting the regime of slavery. Other relevant scholarship includes Foucault, *A History of Sexuality, Vol. 1*; Scott, *Weapons of the Weak*, direct quotation from 34 (emphasis in original), and *Domination and the Arts of Resistance*; Camp, "Pleasures of Resistance," direct quotation from 536, and *Closer to Freedom*.

3. West, "The Debate on the Strength of Slave Families," 238.

4. For further discussion see, White, *Ar'n't I a Woman?*, 70–79; Camp, *Closer to Freedom*, 28–40.

5. See for example Rawick, *American Slave*, 14 (1): 286, 9; 15 (2): 114.

6. Rawick, *American Slave*, 15 (2): 178.

7. Anderson Henderson to John Steele Henderson, 26 January 1849, John Steele Henderson Papers, box 2. series 1.1, fol. 17, 1847–1849, SHC.

8. White, *Ar'n't I a Woman?*, 70–71.

9. Patrol regulations for the county of Rowan; printed by order of the county court at August term, anno domini 1825, www.docsouth.unc.edu/nc/rowan/rowan.html, (10 March 2003).

10. Rawick, *American Slave*, 14 (1): 64 (emphasis added).

11. Jacobs, *Incidents in the Life*, 55.

12. Extracts from the Act of Assembly concerning the duties and privileges of patrols, 1794, chapter 4, www.docsouth.unc.edu/nc/rowan/rowan.html, (10 March 2003).

13. Rawick, *American Slave*, 14 (1): 93.

14. Ibid. 141.

15. Ibid. 15 (2): 218.

16. See Scott, *Domination and the Arts of Resistance* for further discussion of these hidden transcripts.

17. "Born in Slavery: Slave Narratives from the Federal Writers' Project," Arkansas Narratives, 2 (3), 95, http://memory.loc.gov/ammem/snhtml/snhome.html.

18. For an interesting discussion of the concept of honor in African history see, Iliffe. *Honor in African History*

19. Rawick, *American Slave*, 15 (2): 321.

20. Ibid. 14 (1): 69.

21. Interview with Leon Berry, Long Creek, North Carolina, Glenn Hinson Collection, SFC.

22. Ibid.

23. Levine, "Some Go Up and Some Go Down," 71.

24. Interview with Leon Berry, Long Creek, North Carolina, Glenn Hinson Collection, SFC.

25. Frederick Douglass, *Narrative of the Life*, 107

26. Brickell, *The Natural History of North Carolina*, 275 (emphasis added).

27. John F. Thompkins, M.D, "The Management of Negroes," cited in Breeden, *Advice among Masters*, 259.

28. See Sarah F. Hicks Williams to Mr. and Mrs. Samuel Hicks, 18 November 1853, Sarah F. Hicks Williams Letters, 1836–1868, fol. 4, 1853, SHC.

29. Larry Hudson has argued in *To Have and To Hold* that the task system as it operated in antebellum South Carolina allowed the enslaved more autonomy than those who were enslaved outside of the task system, because it provided them with the time and means to work for themselves, cultivating their own plots of land in order to sell their produce and accumulate certain goods for themselves. Hudson further suggested that the garden system facilitated the development of the slaves' internal economy largely of their own making, "the slaves' increasing economic independence facilitated the development of real 'space' between their world and that of the masters wherein they could enjoy a level of cultural autonomy"(20). The picture that emerges from the North Carolina narratives is that the ownership and maintenance of a garden patch was a family duty among the enslaved. Men and women from the same families worked their gardens together, and although they may have divided certain tasks between themselves on the basis of gender, there seems to have been little gender differentiation in terms of actual ownership. Alternatively, other aspects of the informal economy, such as the sale of charcoal which may have resulted in the enslaved having to leave the plantation in order to exchange such goods at market, seemed to have been undertaken by men, as opposed to the weaving of cloth or the sewing of clothes, which was regarded as a woman's duty.

30. Rawick, *American Slave*, 14 (1): 93.

31. Ibid. 188.

32. Ibid.

33. Rawick, *American Slave*, 15 (2): 56.

34. Ibid. 14 (1): 188.

35. Blassingame, "Status and Social Structure in the Slave Community."

36. Rawick, *American Slave*, 15 (2): 114.

37. Ibid. 14 (1): 169.

38. Ibid. 15 (2): 179.

39. Ibid. 14 (1): 188.

40. *Narrative of Lunsford Lane*, 12, electronic edition. This work is the property of the University of North Carolina at Chapel Hill. It may be used freely by individuals for research, teaching, and personal use as long as this statement of availability is included in the text, http://docsouth.unc.edu/neh/lanelunsford/lane.html.

41. For a consideration of the role of hunting in the lives of the enslaved, see Proctor, *Bathed in Blood*, chapter 7, "Slave Perceptions of the Hunt."

42. Rawick, *American Slave*, 14 (1): 2–3.

43. Ibid. 15 (2): 277.

44. Ibid. 14 (1): 199–200.

45. Proctor, *Bathed in Blood*, 157–58.

46. Rawick, *American Slave*, 14 (1): 101 (emphasis added).

47. Ibid.

48. Ibid. 282.

49. Ibid. 387.

50. Ibid. 388.

51. Ibid. 15 (2): 165–66.

52. Ibid. 14, (1): 388.

53. Schipper, *Imagining Insiders*, chapter 7, "Emerging from the Shadows: Changing Patterns in Gender Matters," 130.

54. Ibid. 131.

55. For a discussion of the origins of enslaved folklore, see A. J. Gerber, "Uncle Remus Traced to the Old World"; Brookes, *Joel Chandler Harris, Folklorist*; Crowley, "Negro Folklore: An Africanist View"; Baer, *Sources and Analogues of the Uncle Remus Tales*. For a discussion of African folklore for comparison, see Dayrell, *Folk Stories from Southern Nigeria, West Africa*; Nassau, *Where Animals Talk*; Rattray, *Akan-Ashanti Folktales*; Jablow, *An Anthology of West African Folklore*.

56. Cited in Levine, *Black Culture and Black Consciousness*, 111.

57. Ibid.

58. Harris, "Brother Rabbit's Courtship." *Daddy Jake the Runaway*, 137–45, quote from 145. For a discussion of the methodological problems with these sources see Harris, *The Life and Letters of Joel Chandler Harris*; Brookes, *Joel Chandler Harris, Folklorist*. For an interesting discussion of the ways that the white South read and understood these tales in the postemancipation period, see Ritterhouse, "Reading, Intimacy, and the Role of Uncle Remus in White Southern Social Memory."

59. Beaucatcher \Beau"catch'er\, n. A small flat curl worn on the temple by women. [Humorous] (Webster, 1913). In the *Selma Morning Reporter*, in 1862, the question was posed thus: "Beau-Catchers—A young gentleman friend of ours, who is just 'setting out,' is somewhat curious to know why some young ladies wear what are called beau-catchers—those beautifully curled little locks of hair which adorn their foreheads or temples—He wonders whether every young lady who wears one of them really wants to catch a beau. We wish some one who knows would tell us about it, so we could satisfy his curiosity," 18 December 1862, 1, c. 5, http://www.uttyl.edu/vbetts/selma_al_morning_reporter_1862-1864.htm (15 July 2005).

60. Harris, "Why Brother Bull Growls and Grumbles," *Uncle Remus and His Friends*, 81–90, 83.

61. See Jones, *Labor of Love, Labor of Sorrow*, chapter 1, "My Mother Was Much of a Women: Slavery"; Perrin, "Slave Women and Work in the American South." For a discussion of the ways in which the enslaved made use of the skills of family members in the context of their daily lives see Hudson, *To Have and To Hold*, esp. chapter 2, "The Family as an Economic Unit."

62. Harris, "The Little Boy and His Dogs." *Daddy Jake the Runaway*, 64–74, quotes from 65, 66, 74.

63. Harris, "Uncle Remus's Wonder Story." *Daddy Jake the Runaway*, 98–106.

64. Harris, "The Man and the Wild Cattle." *Uncle Remus and His Friends*, 91–100.

65. Harris, "Brother Fox, Brother Rabbit, and King Deer's Daughter," *Nights with Uncle Remus*, 68–74, 70.

66. See, McLaurin, *Celia*.

67. Hardy Hardison to William Pettigrew, 11 February 1858, Pettigrew Family Papers, box 10, fol. 209, February 1858. SHC. Note that in Hardy Hardison's letter to William Pettigrew he calls the slave in question "Ganzy" while the judicial records referred to "Gauzey." We may probably account for this in terms of Hardy Hardison's misunderstanding of the name in question. For further reference see Catterall, [ed.], *Judicial Cases Concerning American Slavery and the Negro, Volume II*, 215.

68. Jane Caroline (Carey) North to "Louise," 14 February 1858. Ibid.

69. Rawick, *American Slave*, 15 (2): 46.

70. Ibid. 49.

71. See Catterall, [ed.], *Judicial Cases, Vol. II*, 215.

72. Rawick, *American Slave*, 15 (2): 49.

73. Dave Lawson's narrative provides no date for these events, nor the specific county in which they took place, although he does mention that Norwood lived near the Virginia line, "'tween Red Bank and Blue Wing.' He owned lan' 'cross de No'th Carolina line too an' lived close to Blue Wing"(45). We do know that Cleve and Lissa were his grandparents and this therefore suggests that the events described had occurred in the early antebellum period, or at an even earlier date. However, despite extensive searching of the records, including Catterall, [ed.], *Judicial Cases Concerning American Slavery and the Negro, Volume II*; and the web resource, "Documenting the American South," www.docsouth.unc.edu/, I was unable to find any such evidence relating to the case.

Chapter 5. A Red Satin Ribbon Tied around My Finger: The Meaning of the Wedding Ceremony

1. Rawick, *American Slave*, 14 (1): 286–88. The "shoat" that was killed for Tempie and Exter's wedding celebrations refers to a newly weaned piglet.

2. White and White, *Stylin'*, 32.

3. *Aunt Sally or Cross the Way of Freedom*, SCL, 51.

4. Rawick, *American Slave*, 14 (1): 84.

5. "Born in Slavery: Slave Narratives from the Federal Writers' Project," Texas Narratives, 16 (1), 75, http://memory.loc.gov/ammem/snhtml/snhome.html.

6. Rawick, *American Slave*, 15 (2): 374.

7. Ibid. 14 (1): 188.

8. Ibid. 96.

9. "Born in Slavery: Slave Narratives from the Federal Writers' Project," Georgia Narratives, 4 (4), 189–90, http://memory.loc.gov/ammem/snhtml/snhome.html.

10. "Born in Slavery: Slave Narratives from the Federal Writers' Project," Georgia Narratives, 4 (1), 127–28, http://memory.loc.gov/ammem/snhtml/snhome.html.

11. Yetman, *Voices from Slavery*, 306.

12. Rawick, *American Slave*, 14 (1): 84

13. Ibid. 288.

14. Ibid. 287.

15. Ibid. 15 (2): 146 (emphasis added).

16. Ibid. 139–40 (emphasis added).

17. Ibid. 422 (emphasis added).

18. Ibid. 14 (1): 287.

19. Ibid. 15 (2): 422.

20. Cited in Gutman, *The Black Family*, 15.

21. Rawick *American Slave*, 15 (2): 195.

22. Schwalm, *A Hard Fight for We*. 243–46.

23. Sidney Bumpas to Frances Webb, 24 January 1848, Bumpas Family Papers, series one, correspondence, SHC. The underscored space between "blue" and "pantaloons" is in the original source.

24. *Aunt Sally or Cross the Way of Freedom*, SCL, 52–53.

25. Gillis, *For Better, For* Worse, 7.

26. For a discussion of the significance of the links among clothing, identity, and race in the Americas, see Earle, "Two Pairs of Pink Satin Shoes!!" Kirsten Fischer suggests that in colonial North Carolina the practice of keeping one's slaves in minimal clothing encouraged slaveholders to believe that African Americans as a group had inherently different physical needs and sensibilities than even white servants, who through the law were able to demand a certain level of comfort and warmth from the clothing their master provided. The near nakedness of some slaves furthered the idea of the innate differences between black and white in the colonial world. "Believing that slaves were unfazed by their exposure to whites and to each other, white observers saw slaves' near nakedness as a sign of their unrefined sensibilities, their proximity to 'nature' and hence distance from white 'culture,'" (163). See Fischer, *Suspect Relations*, 161–64.

27. See Parker and Warner, "Slave Clothing and Textiles in North Carolina."

28. Jacobs, *Incidents in the Life*, 15.

29. Rawick, *American Slave*, 14 (1): 67–68.

30. Beckles, *Natural Rebels*, 40–41.

31. Camp, *Closer to Freedom*, 57.

32. Albert, *House of Bondage*, electronic addition. This work is the property of the University of North Carolina at Chapel Hill. It may be used freely by individuals for research, teaching, and personal use as long as this statement of availability is included in the text, http://docsouth.unc.edu/neh/albert/menu.html, 20.

33. White and White, *Stylin'*, 27.

34. Rawick, *American Slave*, 15 (2): 74 (emphasis added).

35. Ibid. 14 (1): 84.

36. H. N. McTyiere, "Plantation Life—Duties and Responsibilities," 29, *De Bow's Review*, (September 1860), 357–68, 358–59, University of Michigan: Making of America Project, http://name.umdl.umich.edu/acg1336.1-10.006.

37. C [arter] H[ill], "On the Management of Negroes, Addressed to the Farmers and Overseers of Virginia," cited in Breeden, *Advice among Masters*, 32.

38. Southron, "The Policy of the Southern Planter," cited in Ibid. 243.

39. Cited in Weld, *American Slavery as It Is*, 95.

40. An Overseer, "On the Conduct and Management of Overseers, Driver, and Slave," cited in Breeden, *Advice among Masters*, 151.

41. "Rules of the Plantation," cited in Ibid. 153 (emphasis in original).

42. Sarah F. Hicks Williams to Mr. and Mrs. Samuel Hicks, 10 December 1853, Sarah F. Hicks Williams Letters, fol. 4, 1853, SHC (emphasis added).

43. Cited in Breeden, *Advice among Masters*, 156.

44. Sarah F. Hicks Williams to Mr. and Mrs. Samuel Hicks, 22 October 1853, Sarah F. Hicks Williams Letters, fol. 4, 1853, SHC.

45. Botkin, *Lay My Burden Down*, 64.

46. "Born in Slavery: Slave Narratives from the Federal Writers' Project," South Carolina Narratives, 14 (2), 52, http://memory.loc.gov/ammem/snhtml/snhome.html.

47. "Born in Slavery: Slave Narratives from the Federal Writers' Project," South Carolina Narratives, 14 (2), 127–28, http://memory.loc.gov/ammem/snhtml/snhome.html.

48. "Born in Slavery: Slave Narratives from the Federal Writers' Project," Georgia Narratives, 4 (4), 124, http://memory.loc.gov/ammem/snhtml/snhome.html.

49. Rawick, *American Slave*, 14 (1): 386–87.

50. Ibid. 15 (2): 165.

Conclusion

1. Rawick, American Slave, 14 (1): 118.

2. Ibid. 102.

3. Ibid. 14 (1): 384.

4. Ibid. 283.

5. Maya Angelou, sourced at *About Women's History*, http://womenshistory.about.com/cs/quotes/a/qu_maya_angelou.htm.

Bibliography

Primary Sources

Manuscripts

Southern Historical Collection, Wilson Library, University of North Carolina, Chapel Hill.
Bumpas Family Papers.
Burgwyn Family Papers, 1787–1987.
Cameron Family Papers, 1757–1978
John Steele Henderson Papers, 1846–1916.
James Jones Philips Papers, 1814, 1832–1892.
Lenoir Family Papers, 1763–1936.
Pettigrew Family Papers, 1685, 1776–ca.1939.
Sawyers Creek Baptist Church Records, Camden County, Vol. 1, 31 July 1815–13 November 1853.
Sarah F. Hicks Williams Letters, 1836–1868.
Wheelers (Wheeleys) Baptist Church Minute Book, Vol. 1, 1791–1845, Vol. 2, 1846–1898.

Southern Folklore Collection, University of North Carolina, Chapel Hill.
Glenn Hinson Collection, (1980).

Rare Book, Manuscript and Special Collections Library, Duke University, Durham, North Carolina.
Brickell, John. *The Natural History of North Carolina with an Account of the Trade, Manners, and Customs of the Christian and Indian Inhabitants.* Dublin: James Carson, 1717.
Christian Almanac for North Carolina, 1832.
Cronly Family Papers, 1806–1944.
Davidson Family Papers, 1748–1887.
Devereux Family Papers, 1776–1936.
Francis Cope Yarnell Papers, 1853–1861.
Jones, Charles Colcock. *Negro Myths from the Georgia Coast, Told in the Vernacular.* Cambridge, Mass: Riverside Press, 1888.
Jones, Charles Colcock. Thirteenth Annual Report of the Association for the Religious Instruction of the Negroes in Liberty Co. Georgia, 1848.
McRae Plantation Memorandum Book, 1792–1878.
Thomas and Mary Bingham Lynch Papers, 1794–1895.
Warren, Edward. *A Doctor's Experience in Three Continents: In a Series of Letters Addressed to John Morris M.D of Baltimore*, 1885.

Weld, Theodore. *American Slavery as It Is: A Testimony of a Thousand Witnesses.* New York: American Anti-Slavery Society, 1839.

Williams, Isaac. *Aunt Sally or Cross the Way of Freedom: A Narrative of the Slave Life and Purchase of the Mother of Rev. Isaac Williams of Detroit.* American Reform Tract and Book Society, 1858.

Worth Family Papers, 1844–1955.

Published Primary Sources

Battle, William, ed. *Memories of an Old-Time Tar Heel.* Chapel Hill: University of North Carolina Press, 1945.

Bibb, Henry. "Narrative of the Life and Adventures of Henry Bibb, an American Slave, Written by Himself (1849). In *Slave* Narratives, ed. William L. Andrews and Henry Louis Gates Jr. New York: Library Classics of the United States, 2000.

Botkin, B. A., ed. *Lay My Burden Down: A Folk History of Slavery.* Chicago: University of Chicago Press, 1945.

Breeden, James O., ed. *Advice among Masters: The Ideal in Slave Management in the Old South.* Westport, Conn: Greenwood Press, 1980.

Cameron, Rebecca. "Christmas on an Old Plantation." *Ladies Home Journal* 9 (December 1891): 5–6.

Dayrell, Elphinstone. *Folk Stories from Southern Nigeria, West Africa.* London, New York, Bombay, Calcutta: Longmans Green and Co., 1910.

Douglass, Frederick. *Narrative of the Life of Frederick Douglass, an American Slave* (1845). New York: Penguin Books, 1986.

Escott, Paul D. *Slavery Remembered: A Record of Twentieth-Century Slave Narratives.* Chapel Hill: University of North Carolina Press, 1979.

Grandy, Moses. "Narrative of the Life of Moses Grandy." In *North Carolina Slave Narratives,* ed. William L. Andrews. Chapel Hill, London: University of North Carolina Press, 2003.

Harris, Joel Chandler. *Nights with Uncle Remus: Myths and Legends of the Old Plantation.* Boston, New York: Houghton Mifflin Co., 1883.

———. *Daddy Jake the Runaway and Short Stories Told after Dark by Uncle Remus.* New York: Century Co., 1889.

———. *Uncle Remus and His Friends: Old Plantation Stories, Songs and Ballads with Sketches of Negro Character.* Boston, New York: Houghton Mifflin Co., 1892.

Jablow, Alta. *An Anthology of West African Folklore with an Introduction by Paul Goodman.* London: Thames & Hudson, 1961.

Jacobs, Harriet. *Incidents in the Life of a Slave Girl— Written by Herself, c. 1861.* New York: Dover, 2001.

Jefferson, Thomas. "Notes on the State of Virginia" (1787). Extract reprinted in *Race and the Enlightenment,* ed. Emanuel C. Eze. Oxford: Blackwell Press, 1997.

Jones, Thomas H. "The Experience of Rev. Thomas H. Jones Who Was a Slave for Forty-Three Years." In *North Carolina Slave Narratives,* ed. William L. Andrews. Chapel Hill, London: University of North Carolina Press, 2003.

Ligon, Richard. *A True and Exact History of the Island of Barbadoes.* London: 1673.

Long, Edward. *The History of Jamaica, 3 Volumes.* London: Lowndes, 1774.

Nassau, Robert H. *Where Animals Talk— West African Folklore Tales.* Boston, Fairseas Press, 1912.

Olmstead, Frederick Law. A *Journey in the Seaboard Slave States 1853–4*. New York: Dix & Edwards, 1856.

Rattray, R. S. *Akan-Ashanti Folktales*. Oxford: Clarendon Press, 1930.

Rawick, George P., ed. *The American Slave: A Composite Autobiography*. Vol. 1, "From Sundown to Sunup: The Making of a Black Community." Westport, Conn.: Greenwood Press, 1972.

———, ed. *The American Slave: A Composite Autobiography*. Vol. 14. Westport, Conn.: Greenwood Press, 1972.

———, ed. *The American Slave: A Composite Autobiography*. Vol. 15. Westport, Conn.: Greenwood Press, 1972.

Yetman, Norman. *Voices from Slavery: 100 Authentic Slave Narratives*. New York: Dover Publications, 1970, 2000.

Internet Resources

Albert, Octavia V. Rogers. *The House of Bondage, or, Charlotte Brooks and Other Slaves, Original and Life Like, As They Appeared in Their Old Plantation and City Slave Life; Together with Pen-Pictures of the Peculiar Institution, with Sights and Insights into Their New Relations as Freedmen, Freemen, and Citizens*. New York: Hunt and Eaton, 1890. *Documenting the American South*. 2000. University Library. University of North Carolina at Chapel Hill. 10 February 2006. http://docsouth.unc.edu/neh/albert/menu.html.

A Mississippi Planter. "Management of Negroes upon Southern Estates." *De Bow's Review* 10 (June 1851): 621–27. University of Michigan: Making of America Project. http://name.umdl.umich.edu/acg1336.1-10.006.

Angelou, Maya. *About Women's History*. http://womenshistory.about.com/cs/quotes/a/qu_maya_angelou.htm.

"Born in Slavery: Slave Narratives from the Federal Writers' Project, 1936-1938." http://memory.loc.gov/ammem/snhtml/snhome.html.

Cocke, St. George. "Plantation Management—Police." *De Bow's Review* 14 (February 1853): 177–78, University of Michigan: Making of America Project. http://name.umdl.umich.edu/acg1336.1-14.002.

Extracts from the Act of Assembly Concerning the Duties and Privileges of Patrols, Act 1794. Salisbury, N.C.: *Documenting the American South*. 2001. University Library. University of North Carolina at Chapel Hill. 6 March 2007. www.docsouth.unc.edu/nc/rowan/rowan.html.

Felton, Rebecca Latimer. *Country Life in Georgia in the Days of My Youth*. Atlanta, Ga.: Index Printing Company, 1919. *Documenting the American South*. 1997. University Library. University of North Carolina at Chapel Hill. 8 August 2006. http://docsouth.unc.edu/fpn/felton/felton.html.

Finley, Anthony. Map of North Carolina, 1831. The David Rumsey Map Collection. 27 September 2006. www.davidrumsey.com.

Lane, Lunsford. *Narrative of Lunsford Lane, Formerly of Raleigh, NC, Embracing an Account of His Early Life, the Redemption of Himself and Family from Slavery, and His Banishment from the Place of His Birth for the Crime of Wearing a Colored Skin*. Boston: J. G. Torrey, 1842. *Documenting the American South*. 1999. University Library. University of North Carolina at Chapel Hill. 8 August 2006. http://docsouth.unc.edu/neh/lanelunsford/lane.html.

Macon, T. J. *Life Gleanings*, Richmond, Va.: W. H. Adams, 1913. *Documenting the American South*. 1996. University Library. University of North Carolina at Chapel Hill. 9 March 2007. http://docsouth.unc.edu/fpn/macon/macon.html.

McTyiere, H. N. "Plantation Life—Duties and Responsibilities." *De Bow's Review* 29 (September 1860), 357–68, 358–59. University of Michigan: Making of America Project. http://name.umdl.umich.edu/acg1336.1-10.006.

Oldpoetry.com. http://oldpoetry.com/authors/Thomas%20Campbell.

Page, Thomas Nelson. *Social Life in Old Virginia before the War*. New York: Charles Scribner's Sons, 1897. *Documenting the American South*. 1998. University Library. University of North Carolina at Chapel Hill. 5 March 2007. http://docsouth.unc.edu/southlit/pagesocial/page.html.

Parker, Allen. *Recollections of Slavery Times*. Worcestershire, Mass.: Chas W. Burbank and Co., 1895. *Documenting the American South*. 2000. University Library. University of North Carolina at Chapel Hill. 5 March 2007. http://docsouth.unc.edu/neh/parker/parker.html.

Patrol Regulations for the County of Rowan; Printed by Order of the County Court at August Term, Anno Domini 1825. Salisbury, N.C.: *Documenting the American South*. 2001. University Library. University of North Carolina at Chapel Hill. 6 March 2007. www.docsouth.unc.edu/nc/rowan/rowan.html.

"Selma Morning Reporter." *University of Texas at Tyler*. 15 July 2005. http://www.uttyl.edu/vbetts/selma_al_morning_reporter_1862-1864.htm.

Weston, P. C. "Management of a Southern Plantation: Rules Enforced on the Rice Estate of P. C. Weston, Esq., of South Carolina." *De Bow's Review* 22, (January 1857): 38–44. University of Michigan: Making of America Project. http://name.umdl.umich.edu/acg1336.1-22.001.

Secondary Sources

Books

Baer, Florence E. *Sources and Analogues of the Uncle Remus Tales*. Helsinki: Suomalainen Tiedeakatemia, 1980.

Ball, Edward. *Slaves in the Family*. Harmondsworth: Penguin Books, 1998.

Beckles, Hilary McD. *Natural Rebels: A Social History of Enslaved Black Women in Barbados*. London: Zed Books, 1989.

Blassingame, John W. *The Slave Community: Plantation Life in the Antebellum South*. New York, Oxford: Oxford University Press, 1972.

Brookes, Stella Brewer. *Joel Chandler Harris, Folklorist*. Athens, Ga.: University of Georgia Press, 1950.

Brown, Kathleen M. *Good Wives, Nasty Wenches, and Anxious Patriarchs: Gender, Race, and Power in Colonial Virginia*. Chapel Hill, London: University of North Carolina Press, 1996.

Burton, Orville Vernon. *In My Father's House Are Many Mansions: Family and Community in Edgefield, South Carolina*. Chapel Hill, London: University of North Carolina Press, 1985.

Camp, Stephanie M. H. *Closer to Freedom: Enslaved Women and Everyday Resistance in the Plantation South*. Chapel Hill, London: University of North Carolina Press, 2004.

Cary, Lorin Lee, and Marvin L. Michael Kay, *Slavery in North Carolina 1748–1775*. Chapel Hill, London: University of North Carolina Press, 1995.

Catterall, Helen, ed. *Judicial Cases Concerning American Slavery and the Negro, Volume II, Cases from the Courts of North Carolina, South Carolina, and Tennessee*. New York: Octagon Books, 1968.

Censer, Jane Turner. *North Carolina Planters and Their Children*. Baton Rouge: Louisiana State University Press, 1984.

Davis, Angela. *Women, Race and Class*. New York: Vintage Books, 1981.

Degler, Carl N. *At Odds: Women and the Family in America from the Revolution to the Present*. New York, Oxford: Oxford University Press, 1980.

Dirks, Robert. *The Black Saturnalia: Conflict and Its Ritual Expression on British West Indian Plantations*. Gainesville, Fla.: University of Florida Press, 1987.

Dunaway, Wilma A. *The African-American Family in Slavery and Emancipation*. Cambridge: Cambridge University Press, 2003.

Dusinberre, William. *Them Dark Days: Slavery in the American Rice Swamps*, Oxford, New York: Oxford University Press, 1996.

Faulkner, William. *Absalom, Absalom!* London: Chatto & Windus, 1969.

Fett, Sharla M. *Working Cures: Healing, Health, and Power on Southern Slave Plantations*. Chapel Hill, London: University of North Carolina Press, 2002.

Fischer, Kirsten. *Suspect Relations: Sex, Race, and Resistance in Colonial North Carolina*. Ithaca, London: Cornell University Press, 2002.

Fliegelman, Jay. *Prodigals and Pilgrims: The American Revolution against Patriarchal Authority, 1750–1800*. Cambridge, London, New York: Cambridge University Press, 1982.

Foucault, Michel. *The History of Sexuality, Volume One, An Introduction*, trans. Robert Hurley. London: Penguin Press. 1990.

Fox-Genovese, Elizabeth. *Within the Plantation Household: Black and White Women of the Old South*. Chapel Hill, London: University of North Carolina Press, 1988.

Frazier, E. Franklin. *The Negro Church in America, 1894–1962*. Liverpool: University of Liverpool Press, 1964.

Frey, Sylvia R., and Betty Wood. *Come Shouting to Zion: African American Protestantism in the American South and the Caribbean*. Chapel Hill, London: University of North Carolina Press, 1998.

Genovese, Eugene D. *The World the Slaveholders Made: Two Essays in Interpretation*. New York: Random House, 1969.

———. *Roll Jordan Roll: The World the Slaves Made*. New York: Vintage Books, 1976.

Gillis, John R. *For Better, For Worse: British Marriage from 1600 to the Present*. Oxford: Oxford University Press, 1985.

Gutman, Herbert G. *The Black Family in Slavery and Freedom, 1750–1925*. New York: Vintage Books, 1976.

Hadden, Sally E. *Slave Patrols: Law and Violence in Virginia and the Carolinas*. Cambridge, Mass., London: Harvard University Press, 2001.

Hodes, Martha. *White Women, Black Men: Illicit Sex in the Nineteenth-Century South*. New Haven: Yale University Press, 1997.

Harris, Julia Collier. *The Life and Letters of Joel Chandler Harris*. London: Constable and Co, 1919.

Hudson, Larry E., ed. *Working Toward Freedom: Slave Society and Domestic Economy in the American South.* New York: University of Rochester Press, 1994.

———. *To Have and To Hold: Slave Work and Family Life in Antebellum South Carolina.* Athens, Ga.: University of Georgia Press, 1997.

Hurston, Zora Neale. *Their Eyes Were Watching God.* London: Virago, 1986.

Iliffe, John. *Honor in African History.* Cambridge: Cambridge University Press, 2005.

Johnson, Guion Griffis. *Ante-Bellum North Carolina: A Social History.* Chapel Hill: University of North Carolina Press, 1937.

Jones, Jacqueline. *Labor of Love, Labor of Sorrow: Black Women, Work, and the Family from Slavery to the Present.* New York: Basic Books, 1985.

Joyner, Charles W. *Down by the Riverside: A South Carolina Slave Community.* Urbana, Chicago: University of Illinois Press, 1984.

Jordan, Winthrop D. *White Over Black: American Attitudes Towards the Negro, 1550–1812.* Chapel Hill, London: University of North Carolina Press, 1968.

Lewis, Jan. *The Pursuit of Happiness: Family and Values in Jefferson's Virginia.* Cambridge: Cambridge University Press, 1983.

Levine, Lawrence W. *Black Culture and Black Consciousness—Afro American Folk Thought from Slavery to Freedom.* Oxford, London, New York: Oxford University Press, 1977.

McLaurin, Melton. *Celia: A Slave, A True Story.* New York: Avon Books, 1991.

Malone, Ann Patton. *Sweet Chariot: Slave Family and Household Structure in Nineteenth-Century Louisiana.* Chapel Hill: University of North Carolina Press, 1992.

Matthews, Donald G. *Religion in the Old South.* Chicago, London: University of Chicago Press, 1977.

McCurry, Stephanie. *Masters of Small Worlds: Yeoman Households, Gender Relations, and the Political Culture of the Antebellum South Carolina Low Country.* New York, Oxford: Oxford University Press, 1995.

Morgan, Jennifer L. *Gender and Reproduction in New World Slavery.* Philadelphia: University of Pennsylvania Press, 2004.

Morrison, Toni. *Beloved.* London: Picador, 1987

Mintz, Steven, and Susan Kellogg, *Domestic Revolutions: A Social History of American Family Life.* New York: Free Press. London: Collier Macmillan, 1988.

Outland, Robert B., III. *Tapping the Pines: The Naval Stores Industry in the American South.* Baton Rouge: Louisiana State University Press, 2004.

Patterson, Orlando. *Rituals of Blood: Consequences of Slavery in Two American Centuries.* New York: Basic Civitas, 1998.

Penningroth, Dylan C. *The Claims of Kinfolk: African American Property and Community in the Nineteenth-Century South.* Chapel Hill: University of North Carolina Press, 2003.

Proctor, Nicolas W. *Bathed in Blood: Hunting and Mastery in the Old South.* Charlottesville, Va.: University of Virginia Press, 2002.

Raboteau, Albert J. *Slave Religion: The "Invisible Institution" in the Antebellum South.* Oxford: University of Oxford Press, 1978.

Rothman, Ellen K. *Hands and Hearts: A History of Courtship in America.* New York: Basic Books, 1984.

Schipper, Mineke. *Imagining Insiders: Africa and the Question of Belonging.* London, New York: Cassell, 1999.

Schwartz, Marie Jenkins. *Birthing a Slave: Motherhood and Medicine in the Antebellum South.* Cambridge, Mass.: Harvard University Press, 2006.

Schwalm, Leslie A. *A Hard Fight for We: Women's Transition from Slavery to Freedom in South Carolina.* Urbana, Chicago: Illinois University Press, 1997.

Scott, James C. *Weapons of the Weak: Everyday Forms of Peasant Resistance.* New Haven: Yale University Press, 1985.

———. *Domination and the Arts of Resistance: Hidden Transcripts.* New Haven: Yale University Press, 1990.

Smith, Mark M. *Mastered by the Clock: Time, Slavery, and Freedom in the American South.* Chapel Hill: University of North Carolina Press, 1997.

Sobel, Mechel. *Trabelin' On: The Slave Journey to an Afro-Baptist Faith.* Westport, Conn.: Greenwood Press, 1979.

Sommerville, Diane Miller. *Rape and Race in the Nineteenth-Century South.* Chapel Hill: University of North Carolina Press, 2004.

Stearns, Peter N., and Jan Lewis, *An Emotional History of the United States.* New York: New York University Press, 1998.

Stone, Lawrence. *The Family, Sex, and Marriage in England 1500–1800.* Harmondsworth, Penguin Books, 1977.

Stowe, Steven M. *Intimacy and Power in the Old South: Ritual in the Lives of the Planters.* Baltimore: John Hopkins University Press, 1987.

Tadman, Michael. *Speculators and Slaves: Masters, Traders, and Slaves in the Old South.* Madison: Wisconsin University Press, 1996.

Taylor, Rosser Howard. *Slaveholding in North Carolina: An Economic View.* Chapel Hill, University of North Carolina Press, 1926.

West, Emily R. *Chains of Love: Slave Couples in Antebellum South Carolina.* Urbana: University of Illinois Press, 2004.

White, Deborah Gray. *Ar'n't I a Woman? Female Slaves in the Plantation South.* New York, London: W. W. Norton, 1985.

White, Shane, and Graham White. *Stylin': African American Expressive Culture from Its Beginnings to the Zoot Suit.* Ithaca: Cornell University Press, 1998.

———. *The Sounds of Slavery: Discovering African American History Through Songs, Sermons, and Speech.* New York: Beacon Press, 2005.

Wood, Betty. *Gender, Race, and Rank in a Revolutionary Age: The Georgia Lowcountry, 1750–1820.* Athens, Ga.: University of Georgia Press, 2000.

Yellin, Jean Fagan. *Harriet Jacobs, A Life: The Remarkable Adventures of the Woman Who Wrote Incidents in the Life of a Slave Girl.* New York: Basic Civitas, 2004.

Articles and Individual Chapters in Edited Collections

Bailey, David Thomas. "A Divided Prism: Two Sources of Black Testimony on Slavery." *Journal of Southern History* 46 (August 1980): 381–404.

Bailey, Kenneth K. "Protestantism and Afro-Americans in the Old South: Another Look." *Journal of Southern History* 41 (1987): 451–72.

Bardaglio, Peter W. "Rape and the Law in the Old South: Calculated to Excite Indignation in Every Heart." *Journal of Southern History* 60 (November 1994): 749–72.

———. "Shamefull Matches: The Regulation of Interracial Sex and Marriage in the South before 1900." In *Sex, Love, Race: Crossing Boundaries in North American History*, ed. Martha Hodes. New York: New York University Press, 1999.

Bauer, Raymond A., and Alice H. Bauer. "Day to Day Resistance to Slavery." *Journal of Negro History* 27 (October 1942), No. 4: 388–419.

Beckles, Hilary McD. "Centering Woman: The Political Economy of Gender in West African and Caribbean Slavery." In *Caribbean Portraits: Essays on Gender Ideologies and Identities*, edited by Christine Barrow. Kingston, Jamaica: Ian Randle, 1998.

Baptist, Edward E. "'Stol' and Fetched Here': Enslaved Migration, Ex-Slave Narratives, and Vernacular History." In *New Studies in the History of American Slavery*, ed. Edward E. Baptist and Stephanie M. H. Camp. Athens, Ga.: University of Georgia Press, 2006.

Blassingame, John W. "Using the Testimony of Ex-Slaves: Approaches and Problems." *Journal of Southern History* 41 (November 1975): 473–92.

———. "Status and Social Structure in the Slave Community: Evidence from New Sources." In *Perspectives and Irony in American Slavery*, edited by Harry P. Owens. Jackson, Miss.: University Press of Mississippi, 1976.

Brown, Steven E. "Sexuality and the Slave Community." *Phylon* 42 (Spring 1981): 1–10.

Burnham, Margaret A. "An Impossible Marriage: Slave Law and Family Law." *Law and Inequality* 5 (1987): 187–227.

Clinton, Catherine. "Southern Dishonour: Flesh, Blood, Rape and Bondage." In *In Joy and in Sorrow: Women, Family, and Marriage in the Victorian South*, edited by Carol Bleser. Oxford: Oxford University Press, 1991.

Crowley, Daniel J. "Negro Folklore: An Africanist View." *Texas Quarterly* 5 (Autumn 1962): 65–71.

Durrill, Wayne K. "Slavery, Kinship, and Dominance: The Black Community at Somerset Place Plantation, 1786–1860." *Slavery and Abolition* 13 (August 1992): 1–19.

———. "Routine of Seasons: Labor Regimes and Social Ritual in an Antebellum Plantation Community." *Slavery and Abolition* 16 (August 1995): 161–87.

Earle, Rebecca. "Two Pairs of Pink Satin Shoes!! Race, Clothing and Identity in the Americas (17th–19th Centuries)." *History Workshop Journal* 52 (2001): 175–95.

Escott, Paul D. "The Art and Science of Reading WPA Slave Narratives." In *The Slave's Narrative*, ed. Charles T. Davis and Henry Louis Gates Jr. Oxford: Oxford University Press, 1985.

Fenn, Elizabeth A. "A Perfect Equality Seemed to Reign: Slave Society and Jonkonnu." *North Carolina Historical Review* 65 (1988): 127–53.

Gerber, A. J. "Uncle Remus Traced to the Old World." *Journal of American Folklore* 6 (October–December 1893): 245–57.

Griffin, Rebecca J. "'Goin' Back Over There to See That Girl': Competing Spaces in the Social World of the Enslaved In Antebellum North Carolina." *Slavery and Abolition* 25 (April 2004): 94–113.

———. "Courtship Contests and the Meaning of Conflict in the Folklore of Slaves." *Journal of Southern History* 71 (November 2005): 769–802.

Johnson, William Courtland. "A Delusive Clothing: Christian Conversion in the Antebellum Slave Community." *Journal of Negro History* 82 (Summer 1997): 298–311.

Kaye, Anthony E. "Neighborhoods and Solidarity in the Natchez District of Mississippi: Rethinking the Antebellum Slave Community." *Slavery and Abolition* 23 (April 2002): 1–24.

Labinjoh, Justin. "The Sexual Life of the Oppressed: An Examination of the Family Life of Ante-Bellum Slaves." *Phylon* 35 (1974): 375–97.

Levine, Lawrence W. "Some Go Up and Some Go Down: The Meaning of the Slave Trickster." In *The Unpredictable Past: Explorations in American Cultural History*, ed. Lawrence Levine. Oxford: Oxford University Press, 1993.

Little, Thomas J. "George Liele and the Rise of Independent Black Baptist Churches in the Lower South and Jamaica." *Slavery and Abolition* 16 (1995): 188–204.

Matthews, Donald G. "The Methodist Mission to the Slaves, 1829–1844." *Journal of American History* 51 (1965): 615–31.

Macmillan, Dougald M. "John Kuners." *Journal of American Folklore* 49 (1926): 53–57.

Minchinton, Walter. "The Seaborne Slave Trade of North Carolina," *North Carolina Historical Review* 71 (January 1994): 1–63.

Morgan, Jennifer L. "Some Could Suckle Over Their Shoulder: Male Travelers, Female Bodies, and the Gendering of Racial Ideology, 1500–1770." *William and Mary Quarterly* 54 (January 1997): 167–92. Also in *New Studies in the History of American Slavery*, ed. Edward E. Baptist and Stephanie M. H. Camp. Athens, Ga.: University of Georgia Press, 2006.

Musher, Sharon Ann. "Contesting 'The Way the Almighty Wants It': Crafting Memories of Ex-slaves in the Slave Narrative Collection." *American Quarterly* 53 (March 2001): 1–33.

Parker, Debra, and Patricia Campbell Warner. "Slave Clothing and Textiles in North Carolina, 1775–1835." In *African American Dress and Adornment: A Cultural Perspective*, ed. Barbara M. Starke, Lillian O. Holloman, Barbara K. Nordquist. Iowa: Kendell/Hunt Publishing Co. 1990.

Pearson, Edward A. "A Countryside Full of Flames: A Reconsideration of the Stono Rebellion and Slave Rebelliousness in the Early Eighteenth-Century South Carolina Lowcountry." *Slavery and Abolition* 17 (1996): 22–50.

Penningroth, Dylan C. "My People, My People: The Dynamics of Community within Southern Slavery." In *New Studies in the History of American Slavery*, ed. Edward E. Baptist and Stephanie M. H. Camp. Athens, Ga.: University of Georgia Press, 2006.

Raboteau, Albert J. "Slave Autonomy and Religion." *Journal of Religious Thought* 38 (1981): 54–64.

Ritterhouse, Jennifer. "Reading, Intimacy, and the Role of Uncle Remus in White Southern Social Memory." *Journal of Southern History* 69 (August 2003): 585–622.

Rothman, Ellen K. "Sex and Self-Control: Middle Class Courtship in America, 1770–1870." *Journal of Social History* 15 (1982): 409–25.

Sommerville, Diane Miller. "The Rape Myth in the Old South Reconsidered." *Journal of Southern History* 61 (August 1995): 481–518.

Spindel, Donna. J. "Assessing Memory: Twentieth-Century Slave Narratives Reconsidered." *Journal of Interdisciplinary History* 27 (Autumn 1996): 247–61.

Stevenson, Brenda. "Distress and Discord in Virginia Slave Families, 1830–1860." In *In Joy and in Sorrow: Women, Family, and Marriage in the Victorian South*, ed. Carol Bleser. Oxford: Oxford University Press, 1991.

Stoler, Ann Laura. "'In Cold Blood': Hierarchies of Credibility and the Politics of Colonial Narratives." *Representations* 37 (Winter 1992): 151–89.

Stowe, Steven M. "The Rhetoric of Authority: The Making of Social Values in Planter Family Correspondence." *Journal of American History* 73 (March 1987): 916–33.

Walvin, James. "Slaves, Free Time and the Question of Leisure." *Slavery and Abolition* 16 (April 1995): 1–13.

West, Emily R. "The Debate on the Strength of Slave Families: South Carolina and the Importance of Cross-Plantation Marriages." *Journal of American Studies* 33 (1999): 221–41.

Wills, Gary. "Did Tocqueville 'Get' America?" *New York Review*, 29 April 2004, 52–56.

Woodward, C. Vann. "History from Slave Sources." *American Historical Review* 79 (1974): 470–81.

Yetman, Norman R. "The Background of the Slave Narrative Collection." *American Quarterly* 19 (1967): 534–53.

Dissertations

Battle, Whitney Ophelia. "A Yard to Sweep: Race, Gender, and the Enslaved Landscape." Ph.D. diss., University of Texas at Austin, 2004.

Nickens, Rodney M. "The Slave Religious Experience in Biracial Protestant Churches in North and South Carolina from 1822 to 1861." Ph.D. diss., Southern Baptist Theological Seminary, U.S.A., 1999.

Parkinson, Ralph T. "The Religious Instruction of Slaves." M.A. diss., University of North Carolina, 1948.

Perrin, Liese, "Slave Women and Work in the American South." Ph.D. diss., University of Birmingham, U.K., 1999.

Smith, Victor C. "Church Organization as an Agency of Social Control: Church Discipline in North Carolina, 1800–1860." Ph.D. diss., University of North Carolina, 1967.

Unpublished Papers

Campbell, John F. "Voicing Slavery: Writing the Caribbean and Its Diaspora in the New Millennium." *Caribbean Voices: Writing the Caribbean and Its Diaspora*, Society for Caribbean Studies Conference, University of Warwick, 2002.

Index

communication, secret, 19, 67, 73
competition, 7, 19, 48–50, 51, 81
conjuration, 19, 49–51
corn shuckings, 19, 51, 58, 59, 60, 81, 100
cotton, 9
courtship: across plantations, 55, 64; and family approval, 46–48; games, 58; as resistance, 20, 69–70
Covington, Tom, 57
Cozart, Willie, 89
Craig, Caleb, 7
Crasson, Hannah, 48–49, 76, 77, 78
Cronly, Michael, 56
Crowder, Zeb, 78
Crump, Bill, 59

Darling, Katie, 6
Darlington County, S.C., 6
Davenport, William, 85, 86
Davidson County, 59
Davis, Lucinda, 49
De Bow's Review, 49, 59, 97
Decatur, Ga., 47
Democracy in America (Tocqueville), 30
Dempse, enslaved man, 28
Denson, Mirana, 3, 101
Devereux, Sarah, 32
Devereux, Thomas, 32
Douglass, Frederick, 17
Dowd, Reverend Squire, 67
Dunn, Lucy Ann and Jim, 48, 67, 79, 101, 103
Dunn, Peterson, 48
Duplin County, 96
Durham, Exter, 55, 88, 91, 92, 101, 103
Durham, Snipes, 88, 90
Durham, Tempie Herndon, 55, 77, 88, 90–91, 92, 93, 95, 101, 103
Durham County, 35

Edgecombe County, 9, 60, 66
Edmund, enslaved man, 28
Eliza, enslaved woman, 41
Ellis, James, 52, 93
enslaved men: defined as childlike, 17, 27, 28, 30; and gender identity, 25–29; role as providers, 20, 76, 78–79; sexual stereotypes of, 17, 29–30, 80
enslaved women, sexual stereotypes of, 17, 22–25, 80
Escott, Paul, 13
Europeans, views of Africans, 22, 23
Evans, Millie, 99

Fairfield, S.C., 99
Falls of Neuse, N.C., 3
Faulkner, William, 11
Fayetteville, N.C., 56, 89
Feaster, Gus, 99
Felton, Rebecca Latimer, 25
Fenn, Elizabeth, 62
Ferbie, mother of Alice Baugh, 60
Fett, Sharla, 49–50, 113n70
Fischer, Kirsten, 120n26
Flint, Dr., 5, 56
Florida, 13
folklore, 51, 80–84
Fort Defiance, N.C., 41
Fourth of July, 60
Franklin County, 56, 69, 72

Gauzey, enslaved man, 85, 86
gender and labor, 25–26
Georgia, 37, 47, 65, 89, 100
Gillis, John, 95
Gladdeny, Pick, 99
Grace, enslaved woman, 44
Grace Methodist Episcopal Church, 43
Grandy, Moses, 33
Green, Henry, 73
Greene County, 65, 98
Gregg, Gilbert, 32
Gregory, Angelica, 45
Gregory, R. M., 45
Guildford, enslaved man, 65
Gutman, Herbert, 33, 110n26

Halifax County, 9, 32, 93
Hall, Thomas, 6
Hanover County, Va., 25
Hargrove, Joseph, 77
Hawley, Francis, 98
Haywood, Alonzo, 3, 87, 103
Haywood, Barbara and Frank, 67, 79–80, 100, 101, 103
Haywood, Willis and Mirana, 3, 101, 103
Henderson, Anderson, 70
Henderson, John, 70
Henry, enslaved man, 55
Henry, Essex, 26
Hepzibah Baptist Church, 44, 45
Herndon, George, 55
Hicks, Sarah F. *See* Williams, Sarah Hicks
Hillsborough, N.C., 39
Hinton, James, 65
History of North Carolina (Brickell), 76

CPSIA information can be obtained
at www.ICGtesting.com
Printed in the USA
FFHW021934041218
49752850-54216FF